The Romantic Period in Music

R. Scott Kellner

Copyright 1976
J. Weston Walch, Publisher
Portland, Maine 04104

Contents

Contents

Introduction

A historical epoch, such as the renaissance or the baroque period, is often looked upon as a bygone era quite apart from our own daily lives. The names themselves have an archaic quality, and the study of a renaissance playwright, such as Shakespeare, or a baroque composer, such as Bach, conjures up images of strange costumes and unfamiliar settings.

This is not true of the romantic period. The study of the romantic period in history is actually a study of our own era. While all historical movements have a continuing influence beyond their own time, there is much more than just "influence" in this case. The romantic period has been enthusiastically revived in the last few years. Interests in cultural, social, and even political spheres are turning back in time instead of moving forward. Here are a few of the elements of romanticism. You will no doubt recognize some of your own vital concerns.

The romantics were uncompromising individualists who believed strongly in the integrity of the individual and in his right to express himself freely and completely. They rebelled against tradition, seeking new ways and methods of living free. Their constant questioning of authority resulted in revolutions in America and Europe and in the establishment of democratic systems. Their continual agitation against slavery brought about its abolition in England, America, and Russia; great American romantics like Emerson and Thoreau spearheaded the abolitionist movement in this country.

The romantics also had a deep concern and love for nature. They rejected the dehumanizing aspects of industrialization, and called for a return to a more natural and wholesome environment. This was the age when communes began; groups of young people sharing the same ideals got together and formed community farms.

Their intense love of nature and life is evident in their deeply emotional music; the romantics left us a legacy of beautiful songs. Many of their compositions stemmed from folk songs and ballads, another aspect of the romantic period that our generation is involved in. A number of nineteenth century composers devoted their lives to collecting and preserving the folk songs of their countries.

The modernity of the romantic composer and his art is probably best seen in our own most popular art: the movies. It was the romantic composer's concept of uniting all the arts that led to the development of the movie. In turn, many filmmakers use nineteenth century compositions, or current music composed in the romantic style, for their movie scores. The popularity of these scores (many become hit songs) indicates that romantic music will continue to be composed for some time yet to come.

When we define romanticism then, we are in many respects defining ourselves and our contemporary culture, perhaps the most important and rewarding thing we can do. From this point of view, a study of nineteenth century romanticism is more than just relevant, it is a study of essential personal values.

Robert Scott Kellner

Introduction

I

The Quest for Freedom

The American Revolution in the 1770s had as much impact on the arts as it had on politics. The rise of democracy in this country brought about a profound change in man's outlook on life. The new American represented the New Man, and the entire Western world, closely watching his progress, was influenced by his individualism and independence. American influence was so great that within a decade of American independence, many monarchies in Europe were in danger of collapsing.

One did fall, in fact: France. In 1789, under the banner of "Liberty, Fraternity, Equality," the French people rebelled against the tyrannies and mismanagement of King Louis XVI, and a new republic was born. The old aristocracy was swept out, feudalism became a thing of the past, and the strong and wealthy middle class took power. Free enterprise gave every man a chance to direct his life towards his own goals. Freedom became a password in politics, religion, economics, and the arts. Even Napoleon Bonaparte, who crowned himself Emperor in 1804, could not stifle this new force of individualism.

Johann Strauss, Jr.

The change did not take place rapidly. Historical epochs seldom move faster than a crawl. The American and French Revolutions, though, underlined the fact that mankind was seeking and gaining greater personal liberty and opportunity.

Like no other artist before him, the romantic was involved in the political, as well as social, movements of his times. He longed for freedom, not only in the arts, but in all institutions. He directed his intellect toward politics as often as toward poetry. In England, Shelley wrote political tracts urging the workers to unite; Wagner became a political exile from Germany because of his radical opinions, and Verdi eventually became a deputy and then a senator in the Italian parliament.

Puccini

These and other romantics cheered on the revolutions in America and France in the last decades of the eighteenth century. They also participated in social reform and revolutions and worked directly to abolish slavery in England, America, and Russia during the nineteenth century.

Manners and Morals

The romantic was a rebel in dress as well as in manner. He established the concept of the bohemian. The back-to-nature movement of today, the rebellious youth, and the change in hair styles and fashions that so vividly mark the 1960s and 1970s, are repetitions of the Age of Romanticism. Even the sexual revolution has its counterpart in the early nineteenth century; composers like Chopin, Liszt, and Wagner shocked the public by their countless love affairs, none of which they tried to conceal. In America, the concept of the commune inspired many young men and women to make it a reality. Nathaniel Hawthorne's *Blithedale Romance,* a book about his experiences at Brook Farm in Massachusetts, reads like a modern novel.

Romantic individualism found its way into all aspects of culture in the nineteenth century. Even ball-room dancing was affected. The polka, mazurka, and especially the waltz, broke up the formal patterns of older dances and brought couples together. The minuet and gavotte of the previous century seldom brought the men into such close and prolonged contact with the women as the waltz.

"Shameful!" many older folks said, when first witnessing a waltz. "The morals of this nation are absolutely going to pot!" Composers like Johann Strauss Sr., and then his son, were considered in league with the devil at first; but they soon brought the people of Vienna, and then Europeans and Americans to their feet. The waltz became so popular that the symphonic composers, beginning with Berlioz, soon added it as a movement within their symphonies.

Literature: The Birth of Romanticism

Music tends to follow literature. Classicism began as a literary movement. The poetry of Alexander Pope and the prose of Samuel Johnson preceded by decades the symphonies of Mozart and Beethoven. Romanticism started as a literary movement, and it was in full flower in literature just when classicism was reaching its peak in music.

Inspired by Jean Jacques Rousseau's intensely autobiographical *Confessions,* writers in Germany, France, and England published imaginative and touching stories, called "romances." These stories explored the passionate nature of man, his loves, hates, hopes, and fears. One of the most famous stories, *The Sufferings of Young Werther,* was written by the German poet Goethe. Almost by itself, this book made fashionable the love-struck young man who turns to nature for solace and cannot escape from his heavy feelings of melancholy.

In Germany in the 1770s, several young writers led by Goethe, wrote poems, books, and plays about love and life that were highly personal and emotional. They unblushingly "unveiled their souls" to the public. Their self-searching and passionate outbursts gave the name *Sturm und Drang* (Storm and Stress) to the period. Goethe's *Young Werther* was the introduction to an even greater and moodier work, *Faust.* The Faustian figure, questing, mystical, and unrepentant, showed that the romantic writer was interested in the psychological aspects of man's nature and the unconscious forces that made him act in a way sometimes contrary to his better reasoning. Simply speaking, he was interested in man's capacity for both good and evil. The story of Faust, as told by Marlowe in the Renaissance era, and retold by the great German poet Goethe, captured the imagination of the romantics more than any other story. A number of composers would write symphonies, waltzes, and operas about Goethe's *Faust*.

The romantics believed that man could learn from external nature, as well as from his own internal nature. Wordsworth said: "One impulse from a vernal wood, May teach you more of man. . .Than all the sages can." The romantic (beginning with Goethe's Werther) sought the peace of nature because he felt within him the more powerful forces of his own being. (The many storm scenes in romantic literature and music represent these passions within man's own nature.) The romantic was constantly seeking to understand these passions, or emotional storms. His excursions into the countryside offered only a temporary escape at best.

The romantic had more than just his own nature to escape from. This was the beginning of the Industrial Age, when people were being replaced by machines. The romantics cried out against this dehumanization process and when the Machine Age continued to grind on despite their protests, they turned to their art as a form of escape. Writers like Sir Walter Scott harked back to earlier times, to the medieval period when gallant knights like Ivanhoe rode off to rescue lovely ladies; or to exotic lands, where Oriental pashas bathed in incense and wore silk gowns; or to nature, where brooks and streams and fields of flowers took man far beyond the troubles of civilization.

England and the Byronic Hero

The main thrust of literary romanticism occurred in England. In 1798, the poets Wordsworth and Coleridge published a small book called *Lyrical Ballads*. Coleridge's "Rime of the Ancient Mariner" is, perhaps, the best known poem from that volume. That poem, and the romantic movement in general, examined the relationship of man to God and nature. The romantics believed that man, God, and nature could be united. Through nature, man could not only discover, but become part of God.

Not all poets held that view. Lord Byron, for one, saw the dark side of nature and found it difficult to accept Wordsworth's philosophy of a beneficent nature. Lord Byron was a very handsome, passionate person with a temperament that brooked no interference. His wild ways made his wife leave him; and when the public was outraged by his behavior and sided with his wife, he left his country, vowing never to return. He went to Italy and then on to Greece, throwing his energies into his writing and into the less poetic political struggles that were taking place on the European continent. While fighting for the independence of Greece, he caught a fever and, at the age of thirty-six, died.

Like the other romantics, Byron expressed his own feelings in his poetry, making his work autobiographical. Many of his poetic characters have his own wild and brooding nature. In his work, the "Byronic Hero" stood apart from other men, alone and isolated. He was bold and defiant, a lover of liberty, and yet moody and sensitive, capable of feeling intense psychological pain. This type of moody, nonconformist figure, like the equally romantic figure of Faust, became a model, not only for other literary creations, but for real people. Many artists, including the composers Schumann, Berlioz, Liszt, and Wagner, patterned their lives to some extent after the Byronic hero. It was like an act for some of them (Franz Liszt, for instance, enjoyed playing such roles), but for others it got out of hand. Robert Schumann's ultrasensitivity would drive him insane, and Wagner's egotism would drive away all his friends.

4

The Titan of Music

In an age of such intense individualism, it is not surprising to find a new breed of artist appearing on the stage. The virtuoso, an artist with great technical skill in the use of a musical instrument, became the superstar of the nineteenth century. Performers like Paganini and Liszt were virtuosos who not only played their instruments better than anybody else, but who played dramatically and with great style. These performers were idolized by their audiences and raised to the stature of heroes.

Not that virtuosity wasn't appreciated before. One of the first great virtuosos in Europe was Girolamo Frescobaldi, who lived and worked in Italy in the sixteenth century. When he was appointed church organist for the grand St. Peter's Cathedral in Rome, 30,000 people came to hear his first performance.

Another Italian composer and performer, Domenico Scarlatti, showed Italy and the world what the harpsichord could do, composing dazzling sonatas for that instrument. And, of course, the young Mozart was an example of the child prodigy, displaying his technique on both the violin and piano.

With the romantic movement, virtuosity became a way of life. The middle class had come to power both politically and financially. Their tastes were not as refined as those of the aristocracy they had replaced. They enjoyed and demanded showmanship and great spectacles. Chopin and Liszt awed Europe with their marvelous piano techniques; Nicolo Paganini made the violin sing like no one else before him; and Giacomo Meyerbeer, whose grand, spectacular operas dominated the European theater for decades, became fabulously wealthy.

New opportunities opened up in the arts. Hector Berlioz and others made conducting an art; the demands of Wagner's operas created a whole host of singing stars, and women were finally given an opportunity to display their talents. The brilliant pianist Clara Schumann led the way to recognition of women's musical artistry.

The Virtuoso

One of the first great virtuosos and composers of the nineteenth century was Ludwig van Beethoven. Beethoven's work forms a bridge that spans both the classical period and the romantic. His early years, devoted to classical forms and techniques, equal Mozart and Haydn at their best. In his later years, though, he came to believe that a musician should express his most fervent feelings about life in his music. His search for new forms and methods almost single-handedly revolutionized the art of music.

His need to express himself in his work (which is the essence of romanticism) made Beethoven expand the old classical forms. He would even, when necessary, abandon them and create new ones. Under his hand, the symphony became more unified; concertos put more emphasis on the solo instrument, advancing the virtuoso; and chamber works became miniature musical dramas, with each instrument "speaking" out its part dramatically and emotionally. It was also Beethoven who composed the first important song cycle, a group of songs based on a series of poems. Schubert, who took his inspiration from Beethoven, would make the art song one of the most popular forms of romantic musical expression.

Most people know the story of Beethoven and how deafness struck him in his thirtieth year. Despite this terrible blow, Beethoven heroically went on to compose some of the greatest masterpieces in music. His compositions, reflecting his gigantic battle with fate, are unforgettable in their vitality and power. His famous *Fifth Symphony,* with its remarkable four-note introduction, symbolizes this persistent and Promethean struggle of man against fate.

"Those notes represent Fate knocking at the door of man," Beethoven said. "And man need not fear to answer; he is the master of his fate."

Many years after Beethoven's death, Franz Liszt, who personifies all that romanticism stands for, wrote, "To us musicians, the work of Beethoven is like the pillars of smoke and fire which led the Israelites through the desert and into the Promised Land. We all follow his light to glory."

The Prince of Song

Franz Schubert, like Beethoven, was both a classicist and a romantic. His symphonic works are mostly classical. His first two symphonies were composed in imitation of Mozart and Haydn. In fact, they are even scored for the same instruments used in Mozart's last symphony. Schubert also experimented with key changes and harmony, and, by the time he wrote his "Unfinished" Symphony, there was a new tonality and chromaticism in his work. It was in this symphony and the one to follow that he expressed his romantic tendencies in music.

Schubert's originality was more evident in his piano pieces than in his orchestral works. He broke free from the sonata form and originated *Moments Musical,* short piano pieces dealing with brief musical thoughts. He created the Impromptu, a form which Chopin and other romantic composers would often use. He also helped establish the waltz as a musical and dance form, inspiring not only Chopin, but Johann Strauss, to make the waltz king of the dances.

It is in the art song, though, that we find Schubert's greatest contribution to romanticism. He wanted to set poems to music, establishing a partnership between language and song. By matching the rhythmic patterns of the words and music, he was able to add another dimension to sound. Schubert was so talented at matching melody and word that his songs became miniature dramas.

Schubert died at the early age of thirty-one, comparatively unrecognized. It wasn't long before he was "discovered." His songs (more than 500 of them) became extremely popular. Before the nineteenth century was over, millions of households would be proud to have his music and songs on their pianos. "Schubert gives wings to the imagination," one romantic composer wrote, "like no other composer save Beethoven."

Freedom from Form

Generally speaking, classicism stresses precision and form. It is an objective art, where the composer controls his emotions and strives to make his work universal, rather than individual.

Romantic music, on the other hand, is composed in broader strokes, with the composer seeking to free himself from restrictive forms. Romantic art is subjective; the composer puts his strongest passions into his music and seeks to make a personal and individual statement.

The individuality that romanticism stresses is apparent in the many different styles in this period. It was an age of great contrasts where form was concerned. Chopin gave the nineteenth century his short, intimate piano pieces, while Liszt exhibited his fiery showpieces; Berlioz expanded the orchestra to add more brilliance and color to his program music, while Brahms brought back the smaller ensemble to play his absolute music; and while Wagner was creating his ultraserious music drama, Offenbach was responding with his lighthearted operettas.

The romantic's love for beautiful, expressive melodies led to a new treatment of melodic themes within a work. In the classical period, themes were usually stated, developed, and then recapitulated (sonata form). Developing a theme meant breaking it down into fragments or modifying it in different ways until the original melody was no longer distinguishable.

The romantics wanted to keep their beautiful melodies more intact. Their technique, known as "Transformation of Themes," was to repeat the theme with various changes in the harmonic coloring, or alterations of the rhythm or intervals. Berlioz called this the "fixed idea," when a theme, representing a particular character or idea, kept appearing and reappearing throughout a work. Later, Wagner would compose entire operas made up of dozens of such themes, called leitmotifs, which were modified according to the dramatic situation on stage.

One of the things that made romantic themes so expressive was a change in concept regarding melody and harmony. A heavy emphasis on chromaticism came into being in the nineteenth century. Chopin, Schumann, and Liszt altered the chords in their harmonic lines to achieve a chromatic harmony. Such alterations in the key added "color" to the work and helped to heighten the emotional tension of their music. Chromaticism is a melodic or chordal tone that is not in the key of the composition. Such chromaticism was employed by the baroque composers in their religious works (it helped express a mood, such as grief) and Mozart used chromaticism sparingly in his compositions. Chopin's and Liszt's use of chromaticism was intrinsic to their work. After they led the way, the other romantics lost no time in exploiting the variety of tone colors that such altered chords brought into music.

This extensive use of chromaticism was the first step in the breakdown of tonality that would lead ultimately to the atonality of the twentieth century. Before romanticism, composers usually modulated into closely related keys when varying their harmonies. Their logic in changing keys was always obvious and incontestable. Romantic composers modulated into new keys that had a distant and not so obvious relationship to the original key. Like chromaticism, this clash of keys helped produce a tension and excitement that the romantics wanted in their work. Dissonance was used as a technique to prolong this tension. As the century progressed, composers moved less quickly to resolve dissonant tones.

The Nationalists

Part of the reason for these changes in melodic and harmonic structures was the new sense of national identity that was emerging among the artists in Europe. Prior to the romantic period, most great composers came from Germany, France, or Italy. Germany and Italy, especially, established the forms that music was to follow for some time.

The new sense of individual freedom that emerged in the nineteenth century inspired composers from all the European nations to challenge the dominance of these forms. Artists became proud and were determined to display the music of their own cultures. From Poland came Chopin, who gave the music world the special rhythms and harmonies of the polonaise and mazurka; Hungary produced Liszt, whose brilliant virtuosity at the piano helped create new fashions; from Russia came the highly melodic Tchaikovsky and the intensely nationalistic Mussorgsky. Later in the century, Grieg would bring the music of Norway to the world; Dvorak would do the same for Bohemia. America, though late in adding names to the musical geniuses of the world, produced Edward MacDowell, whose instrumental, choral, and piano works were the first serious American music to become popular in Europe.

With so many composers contributing music from so many countries, there just had to be great changes in rhythm and harmonic structures. There were also some changes in instrumentation.

The Development of the Orchestra

Romantic composers put the orchestra to maximum use. They liked to "paint" with music. Mendelssohn, for instance, tried to capture the ebb and flow of waves moving in and out of the opening of a dark cavern; Wagner sought to "paint" a raging storm at sea; and Schumann tried to capture the color of a carnival with only a piano!

Such interest in painting musical pictures led them to experiment with different instrument combinations and different instruments. The romantics enlarged the orchestra and added extra instruments to get as much tone color as they could. They improved the French horn, adding valves, so it could play the full chromatic scale; the string instruments were revised to give fuller and louder sounds; and new instruments, such as the tuba, celesta, and saxophone, were invented and placed in the ever-growing orchestra.

As for its size, here is an idea of how the symphony orchestra developed during the romantic period:

Mozart and Haydn (1770)	Berlioz (1830)	Mahler (1900)
20 Strings:	40 Strings:	60 Strings:
violins	violins	violins
violas	violas	violas
cellos	cellos	cellos
basses	basses	basses
1 Flute	2 Flutes	4 Flutes
2 Oboes	2 Oboes	3 Oboes
2 Clarinets	2 Clarinets	3 Clarinets
2 Bassoons	4 Bassoons	2 Bassoons
2 Horns	4 Horns	6 Horns
timpani	timpani	timpani
	1 English horn	1 English horn
	2 Trumpets	4 Trumpets
	3 Trombones	3 Trombones
	2 Tubas	1 Tuba
	Cymbals	Cymbals
	Bass drum	Bass drum
	Piccolo	Contrabassoon
	Cornet	Glockenspiel
	Harp	Triangle
		Gong
		Small drum
		Harp

There was also a new permanence for the orchestral ensemble. Before the romantic period, orchestras were small. Unless they were established by some nobleman for his private use, they were temporary in nature and brought together only for specific occasions.

After 1800, orchestras not only increased in size, but became institutions in themselves. It was in the first half of the nineteenth century that London, Paris, and New York had their own permanent Philharmonic Orchestras. The name "philharmonic" was coined from the two Greek words meaning "love of harmony."

Music as Drama

As romanticism was so fully expressed in literature, romantic composers often wedded their music to literature, giving their compositions more depth and force. They, too, wanted to tell inspiring stories, but in music instead of words.

This program music, as it was called, attempted to paint a picture, tell a story, or describe an idea in musical notes. That might sound like a difficult thing to do, but there are some obvious correspondences between music and the sounds of life. A flute used to imitate the sound of a bird, or a drum to duplicate the pounding of a horse's hoofs are programmatic.

Program music was not new in the 1800s. Haydn was fond of imitating animal sounds with music, and before him, the French composer Clement Janequin "painted" battle scenes and pastoral landscapes with his orchestra.

With Beethoven's *Pastoral Symphony* and Berlioz' *Fantastic Symphony,* program music really came into its own. Berlioz not only gave each movement of his symphony descriptive titles, but he also wrote out a program explaining the music to the audience.

Franz Liszt was influenced by Berlioz to develop the symphonic poem, or "tone poem." This was shorter than a symphony and could tell a story or relate an idea in one movement. His *Les Preludes* is, perhaps, the best known tone poem ever composed, and certainly the most dramatic.

Another popular symphonic poem is *Danse Macabre* by Saint-Saëns, which depicts Death dancing and playing a violin in a graveyard at midnight. It is quite an effective piece of music, as you can imagine.

Romantic Opera

There were many styles of opera in the beginning of the nineteenth century. In Paris, opera was produced on a grand scale. The spectaculars of Meyerbeer were not only enjoyable to hear, but fascinating to look at.

In Italy, composers like Rossini were developing light opera, known as opera buffa (comic opera). These were light in tone, gay in spirit, and always had a happy ending. Rossini was probably the most prolific of all opera composers, writing thirty-eight operas in nineteen years. He used to travel about Italy composing new operas every few months for whomever would commission one. Other important composers of Rossini's time were Donizetti and Bellini, whose works are still performed today.

The greatest Italian composer was Giuseppe Verdi, a nationalist whose patriotic operas helped unite the people of Italy. Verdi's operas were highly melodic, filled with beautiful songs that became "hit tunes" all over Europe.

Nationalism also played a large role in the development of opera in Germany. Composers like Weber early in the century used German legends and folk tales for their librettos. After them came Wagner, who changed everything with his *music dramas* (he didn't call his work opera). Wagner was both a nationalist and an arch-romantic. He was determined to capture the "German spirit" in his music dramas; he carried the romantic's dream of a united art, music, painting, drama, and poetry all combined, to its fullest development. His music dramas united music, words, action, and scenery as no other composer had so far succeeded in doing.

In Russia, too, nationalism played its part. Mussorgsky's *Boris Godunov* represents not only a Russian story, but a serious break with western European concepts of harmony and melody. The strong psychological development of character that makes the Russian novel so outstanding, can also be found in these late Russian operas.

The endurance of nineteenth century operas can be seen each year, when the majority of offerings by most opera companies are still romantic operas. Despite the fact that hundreds of twentieth century operas have been composed and offered to the public, these earlier works continue to dominate the field.

Music as Business

Interest in music became so widespread that it led to the establishment of dozens of institutions, a whole new industry in fact, that handled the ever-increasing demands of the public. Between 1795 and 1870, schools of music were established in France, Prague, Brussels, Vienna, London, and Leipzig. America's first conservatories were Oberlin, New England, and Cincinnati (these three within the space of two years: 1865-67), with many more to follow in the decades to come.

Almost every well-to-do household owned a piano, making that industry very profitable. The accordion, invented in Berlin in the 1820s, was immediately popular, starting yet another industry. The harmonium, a keyboard instrument much like a small piano, but operated by foot bellows, was also sold to many homes.

New publishing firms came into being and many of them made good profits selling keyboard music. Composers were called upon to create exercises and etudes for their pupils to practice. The etudes of Czerny, Chopin, and Liszt became big sellers at the music stalls.

The composer had to depend upon himself for a living. There were no more rich patrons. An occasional composer, like Tchaikovsky, would find a benefactor, but most had to rely on their own resources. There were several ways they could earn a living. Most earned money in the concert halls, either playing or conducting; many taught, as there was no end to the supply of students; and some of them were under contract to publishers, supplying the music for the new wave of students and amateur performers.

The Romantic Artist

With the aristocracy and the church no longer leading patrons of the arts, artists found themselves in a new position. They, too, had to support themselves. They looked around for scenes and themes that they thought might interest the public, and after their pictures were painted, they took them to special exhibitions where they were sold.

Nature scenes appealed to the romantics and to their new clientele. Artists began to take easels and paints outside to capture the freshness and brilliant colors of nature. Before this period, artists made sketches of landscapes and then took them into their studios to paint in the colors. The English artists, Constable and Turner, with their new approach to landscape painting and their efforts to portray the constantly changing aspects of nature, would greatly influence the impressionist movement later in the century.

It was a Spanish painter though, Francisco Goya, who first led the way for the romantic artists. He was a fiery personality who lived through some difficult and anxious times. One day, after Napoleon's army had conquered Spain, Goya came across a terrible scene of death. Spanish patriots had been lined up against a wall and mercilessly murdered by French troops. Shaken by this outrage, the artist dipped his handkerchief in the blood of the dead Spaniards and sketched out the gruesome scene on the wall beside him. Later he would transfer that scene to canvas, creating his most famous work, *The Third of May*. There is almost a primitive quality to this work. It is vivid, forceful, realistic in detail, and yet romantic in its intense expression of emotion.

In his seventy-eighth year, nearly blind and totally deaf, Goya somehow managed to cross the rugged Pyrenees mountains to spend his last days in "the capital of the art world," in France. His presence there inspired the new generation of painters.

Eugene Delacroix, the leader of the French romantic painters, was strongly influenced by Goya and by the writings of Lord Byron. He rejected the conventional and static art of the classicists, preferring the color and drama of the baroque artists, especially Rubens. Many of Delacroix's paintings were like Rubens', large historical scenes full of brilliant color and restless action.

Art critics were somewhat less progressive than literary critics and critics of music. Consequently, Delacroix had a difficult time getting his work accepted. His paintings were always being measured against the classical style of David and Ingres and unhappily, found wanting. But as is so often the case, the critics think one thing and the public another. Delacroix was quite popular. When his intense romanticism helped bring on the movement of impressionism, the critics finally recanted, belatedly admitting the importance of Delacroix's place in the history of art.

No End in Sight

By the end of the nineteenth century, romanticism was losing its hold. Writers and poets had already turned their attention away from the romantic myths and legends to find their stories and ideas in the very realistic present.

Musicians were also turning to realism, especially in the opera. Mascagni, Leoncavallo, and Puccini produced works that inaugurated the *verismo* (realism, truth) movement. Instead of heroic subjects and characters, realistic people were presented in realistic settings.

Though romanticism gave way to a series of other movements at the turn of the century: realism, impressionism, and, eventually, atonalism, romanticism never died out. Throughout the twentieth century romantic music has remained the favorite, both with the public, and with professional musicians. It would appear that no matter what new movements come and go in the arts, romanticism will coexist alongside them, too, forever enjoyable and always in vogue.

Study Activities

1. In the nineteenth century many people patterned their lives after the Byronic hero. How would you define this character? Is this still a popular figure? Who are our "heroes" today? What are their character traits? Are there any "outlaws" among them?

2. Make a list of the great women authors of the nineteenth century and their major works (include poets, essayists, and novelists). What women are comparably famous in the other arts, music and painting? Why are there so few?

3. History is about people. All of the people listed below were mentioned in this chapter. Briefly identify each, writing W for writer, C for composer, or A for artist after each name. Do as many as you can at first without referring back to the chapter.

Beethoven	Hawthorne	Rossini
Bellini	Ingres	Rousseau
Berlioz	Johnson	Rubens
Brahms	Leoncavallo	Saint-Saëns
Byron	Liszt	Schubert
Chopin	MacDowell	Schumann
Coleridge	Marlowe	Scott
Constable	Mendelssohn	Shelley
Czerny	Meyerbeer	Strauss
David	Mozart	Tchaikovsky
Delacroix	Mussorgsky	Turner
Donizetti	Offenbach	Verdi
Dvorak	Paganini	Wagner
Goethe	Pope	Weber
Goya	Puccini	Wordsworth

4. Write a three-page essay on the trend in the arts today. Is it forward looking, or looking back in time? Is there still a close relationship between literature, painting, drama, and music?

5. Romantic music is still being composed, although not for the concert halls. Maurice Jarre's "Doctor Zhivago" and Bennett's "Nicholas and Alexandra" are two movie themes which have become extremely popular. Can you name five other recent movies whose orchestral music has become popular? How important is music in movies?

II

Frederic Chopin:

Poet of the Piano

Frederic Chopin was born on March 1, 1810 in a Polish town a few miles from Warsaw. His father was a French citizen who moved to Poland to teach French to the Polish nobility. He was a cultured man and would soon open a school in Warsaw. Chopin's mother, also highly cultured, was a member of the Polish nobility. Young Frederic would be reared in an atmosphere of learning and refinement.

Chopin's interest in music began early. He enjoyed creating new and beautiful melodies on the family piano. His sister Louise was his first teacher. They played duets together, and the father, who was an amateur violinist, would often join in.

Music became such an important part of Chopin's daily life that he was only seven years old when his first composition, a lively polonaise, was published. Two years later he gave a public performance in Warsaw which was a great success and earned him the nickname, "the Polish Mozart." The nine-year-old boy became famous in the Polish capital overnight and was a frequent guest and entertainer of the Polish nobility.

It was quite remarkable that Chopin seemed to learn the piano almost on his own. His only professional piano teacher was really a violinist. Nevertheless, he instructed the boy as best he could. He also encouraged Chopin to set his own thoughts to music.

Chopin

His most influential teacher was Josef Elsner, the director of the Warsaw Conservatory, who instructed him in composition. When Chopin was fifteen, he began his studies with Elsner. It was a perfect match. Chopin was eager to experiment and Elsner was tolerant enough to let him. He guided Chopin in the development of a unique style, encouraging the young man to put aside classical forms and the classicist's notions of restraint. Chopin was allowed to give his pieces the same romantic expression that the poets and painters were bringing into their art. By the time Chopin was ready to graduate, he had established his own style, one based on sound musical practices. He would be forever grateful to Elsner.

A New Life for Old Dances

As a composer and performer, Chopin was drawn to the other capitals of Europe. Vienna, Paris, and Berlin competed as cultural centers. After visiting Berlin in 1828, where he was greatly stimulated by the musical activity, he was more determined than ever to at least see Vienna and Paris.

After graduating from the Conservatory, Chopin was given the funds by his father to visit Vienna. He arrived there in the summer of 1829. In that year, Chopin joined ranks with the great artists of his time. He gave two concerts in Vienna within the space of one week, and both were highly successful. "We knew you would bring great honor to Poland," his teacher told him upon his return.

The Viennese really enjoyed Chopin's music, especially the Polish dances which seemed to leap up out of his piano by themselves. These were the polonaises and mazurkas, native rhythms of Poland. The first thing that Chopin ever composed was a polonaise (when he was eight). The polonaise orginated as a Polish court dance in the seventeenth century. It is a dance in 3/4 meter and its rhythmic pattern looks like this:

The polonaise is usually a stately dance. But Chopin used it to release the martial element of his temperament. His beloved country was constantly at war with Russia, and his polonaises ring with a military spirit. His *Polonaise in A Major* is even subtitled "Military," and his most famous one in A-flat major is known as "Heroic."

Mazurkas are Polish folk dances, similar in time to the waltz but performed by a group of couples. The accent is on the third beat (it is on the first in a waltz), giving the mazurka a very distinct character. Here is an example of one:

In all, Chopin composed over fifty mazurkas and a dozen polonaises.

Unrequited Love

Chopin decided to move permanently to Vienna in 1830, when he was twenty years old. Leaving his homeland was the most difficult thing he ever had to do. Though in one respect, it was easy for Chopin to leave Warsaw. He had fallen in love with the beautiful Constantia Gladkowska, for whom he composed his beautiful *Piano Concerto in F Minor*. But his love was not returned. Traveling, adventure, and public attention seemed a good way to forget her. Taking leave of Poland and his family was one of the low points in Chopin's life.

Leaving his friend and teacher, Josef Elsner, was equally sad. As a going away present, Elsner gave his pupil a small silver urn containing a handful of dark, rich earth. "Carry this with you always," said the teacher, "and you will be carrying with you a small part of Poland. Never forget your country."

And Chopin never did forget his origins. No matter how successful he became in Vienna and Paris, no matter how great he was the world over, he always thought of Poland, incorporating Polish folk tunes and dances into his many works.

The Concerto

Chopin wrote two piano concertos. The first one is the most popular, but because of the reverse order in which his two concertos were published, the first one is called *Concerto No. 2*.

Chopin had his own idea of what a concerto should be. He did not think, as Beethoven did, that the solo instrument and the orchestra should engage in an "argument" that eventually leads to a reconciliation. Nor did he agree with his friend Liszt that the struggle should be a fierce one, with the solo instrument eventually winning out. Chopin did not think that a concerto should be a struggle for supremacy. The piano was unquestionably supreme as far as he was concerned, and so it could begin immediately to do what it does best, to weave its wonderfully melodic magic. The orchestra was to provide a harmonic, and at times dynamic, background, giving emphasis to the piano's brilliant singing.

Because his works were highly melodic, Chopin considered each movement of his concertos capable of standing on its own. He was not overly concerned with unity between movements. In fact, during the first performance, when he himself played the solo part, he slipped in someone else's music between the first and second movement as a diversion for the audience.

In his F minor concerto, the strings and oboes are used to introduce the two main themes. He employs these instruments masterfully, but when the piano comes in, you know instantly which instrument will rule. In a series of beautiful scales, the piano sings out its melody, concentrating mainly on the first theme.

The second movement, the larghetto, with its tender and nostalgic melody, was obviously composed with Constantia in mind. It is purely romantic in its expression of love and longing, and leads into a very dramatic close, where the violins pulsate in the background while the piano both defiantly and sorrowfully continues to sing.

The concluding movement, a cross between a waltz and a mazurka, fast in tempo and beautiful in development, reaffirms the composer's good spirit.

Chopin did recover rather well from Constantia's rejection. When the *Concerto in F Minor,* which he had composed for her, was finally published (in 1836), Chopin blithely dedicated it to some other woman, a young countess who very easily made him forget poor Constantia.

The National Hero

Once back in Vienna, Chopin scored another success, giving concerts for the public and playing at small affairs. His move to Vienna came at the right time. War broke out between Poland and Russia. In a futile effort, the Poles were trying to get out from under Russian rule. Russia, Prussia, and Austria had taken over Poland in the previous century, dividing the country between them in the 1770s. The Polish nationalists had been trying to get their country back ever since the division.

Chopin, who had a slender frame and fragile health, would have made little difference in the outcome had he enlisted as a soldier and returned home. Instead, he remained in Vienna and placed his patriotic feelings in his music. He wrote the *Etude in C Minor,* the famous "Revolutionary" Etude, and he contributed as much as he could financially to help Poland's cause and to care for the many refugees who were fleeing the country.

His music did contribute a great deal to keep hope and spirit alive. Although he was out of Poland for the last half of his life, Chopin was still considered the Polish national composer. His music meant everything to the Polish people. During the late 1800s, while under the oppressive rule of Czarist Russia, the Polish people were forbidden many things: their language, faith, national dress, and even their folk songs. The Russians were determined to subjugate them completely. But they failed to prohibit Chopin's music, mistakenly thinking he was a French composer. The joy of listening to Chopin's beautiful melodies was enough to keep the Polish spirit alive. "In Chopin," wrote one patriot, "we could still take hope; he was the living breath of freedom."

And again many years later, when the Nazis invaded Poland in 1939, it was Chopin's music that became the symbol of hope and resistance. While the Nazis dropped bomb after bomb on the historic city of Warsaw Chopin's "Revolutionary" Etude, and many of his other songs were broadcast from the Warsaw radio. His was the last music that the Polish people heard before the surrender to Germany.

Such resistance stemmed from the composer himself. In 1837, Chopin received a generous offer from the Russian Czar to be his court pianist. Chopin could have used the money, and the position was extremely prestigious. How did he respond? "You have ruled my beloved Poland," he wrote directly to the Czar, "but never will you rule Frederic Chopin!"

Playing in Paris

Chopin went from Vienna to Paris, expecting to stay there for only a short visit. But he immediately fell in love with what was then, and possibly still is, the most beautiful city in the world. Paris was the center of romanticism, just as Vienna had been the Mecca for the classicists. Chopin soon met such great composers as Liszt, Berlioz, Mendelssohn, and Rossini; literary greats such as Balzac, Dumas, Hugo, Heine, and Sand; and artists of the stature of Delacroix.

But Chopin would have to work hard for his success in Paris. His first concerts were not received with the same admiration he had been given in Vienna. The critics panned his work, accusing him of self-indulgence. They especially didn't like the way he modulated from one key to another or the way he linked his musical phrases together.

There was a time during these first few months in Paris that Chopin got so discouraged he contemplated moving away. He would start life anew, he thought; cut ties with tradition and create his art in an atmosphere best suited to innovation and experimentation. In short, he decided to go to America.

Had it not been for a chance meeting with an old friend one evening, who introduced Chopin into the exclusive circle of the rich and influential Rothschilds, Chopin would have sought his fortune in America. As it was, he was "discovered" by Baron Jacques de Rothschild and was soon the sensation of Paris. Before long he was being asked to perform at the many social functions of the well-to-do; he also received generous fees as a teacher of the piano.

Though he often liked to be alone, and was moody and somewhat self-centered, Chopin enjoyed entertaining at the Paris *salons*, mingling with the famous and the rich. He was an aristocrat by birth, related through his mother to the Polish nobility, and he was unquestionably an aristocrat by inclination. He loved beauty and splendor and hated the mundane. He felt that his newly-found place in high Parisian society was rightly his, and he had no trouble fitting in. "You would think he was born a French nobleman," Franz Liszt remarked.

Competing with Strauss

Chopin's sophisticated waltzes mirror his interest in Parisian high society. At first Chopin did not like waltz music. When he visited Vienna in 1830 and heard the music of Johann Strauss and Joseph Lanner, he complained that they pandered too much to the public and didn't try to bring out the best qualities of the waltz form.

Chopin had composed three waltzes of his own before he went to Vienna, and he did not think he would compose any more. But the insistent rhythm of the waltz is not so easily put aside. After his exposure to the Austrians, he again gave the waltz his artistic attention.

To lessen the heavy quality of the waltz, Chopin adroitly modified the persistent left-hand 3/4 rhythm. In some of his waltzes, he suddenly shifts part of the melody downward into the rhythm section or, as in his *Waltz in A Minor,* brings the rhythm up the keyboard after having begun the melody with the left hand. He also occasionally delayed or even dropped a beat to check the rhythmic impulse.

Chopin wrote two dozen waltzes. The most beautiful—and one of the most popular—is his *Waltz in C-sharp Minor.* It is a very graceful waltz with its thrice-recurring section marked *piu mosso* (increase the tempo) and its concise statement of the main theme. More than any other, this waltz shows how Chopin could take a popular dance and turn it into an aesthetic art form.

And of course there is the "Minute" Waltz, his best known. It is a brief waltz, but it takes *two* minutes to play. The word "minute" here is the French word for "small." The "Minute" waltz is a very fast waltz; no one is likely to dance to it. Yet it is graceful and quite charming.

One critic summed up Chopin's waltzes quite well: "They are not like the waltzes of Johann Strauss. They are not meant to be danced to. Chopin's waltzes are dances for the soul . . . not for the body."

Teacher and Technician

Unlike most of his fellow musicians, Chopin did not enjoy giving concerts or performing before large masses of people. He used to get terribly nervous when he had to give a major concert. He preferred the smaller audience of the *salons,* where he knew almost everybody in the room.

Chopin directed his energies more toward teaching and gave fewer and fewer public performances. He earned enough from teaching (usually four pupils a day) to pay for the expensive clothes and furniture that his aristocratic tastes called for.

Chopin was naturally interested in developing good piano technique in his students, and he wrote many etudes. Etudes are basic pieces to develop the student's playing skills. The word means "study" in French, or "exercise." Most composers have written etudes, some entire series of them. The etudes of Czerny, a contemporary of Chopin's, are still ranked among the most important exercises for modern pianists. Chopin's etudes and exercises in octaves and arpeggios, in thirds and sixths, are not the repetitive, dry stuff that one finds in most studies. In his typical fashion, he turned his etudes into beautifully lyric songs and passionate hymns. His *Etude in E Major,* for instance, composed initially as an exercise in playing double notes, is an example in miniature of the climactic ebb and flow of romantic emotion. Another exciting piece is his *Etude in A Minor,* the "Winter Wind" Etude. The glittering scalework and strong octaves in this exercise has made this a favorite showpiece for concert performers.

Chopin not only wanted to expand his student's potentials, he was also interested in expanding the piano's use and developing its possibilities as a musical instrument. One of his techniques was to set up masses of tone with the left hand, striking widely spaced open chords and sustaining them by careful use of the foot pedal. His frequent use of the pedal to blend the musical tones together achieved a rich fabric of sonorities.

In order to fill the air with as much music as possible, Chopin employed a variety of delicate ornaments, such as grace notes, trills, and sparkling glissandos. His rather dashing use of arpeggios is another feature of his compositions.

To get the piano and his melodies to "sing," Chopin used the technique known as *rubato.* This allowed him to slow down or speed up the melody at will, according to mood, "robbing" time from some beats to add it to others. Occasionally he would use full rubato, used most often by Liszt and Schumann, which let him moderate the tempo of the harmony as well as of the melody.

Chopin had the classicist's love for dynamics. But instead of juxtaposing different sounds for their startling effects, he made his crescendos and decrescendos, his pianissimos and fortissimos an organic part of the work. Though he could, as he does in his "Heroic" Polonaise, employ dynamics with the same startling intensity as Beethoven.

As for his harmony, that differed sharply from previous composers. His use of chromatic chords helped in modulating between keys and in evoking mood. He used discords dramatically, placing them effectively in his marches and polonaises. His experiments with a variety of harmonics enabled him to obtain color effects and sonorities that were both pleasing and emotionally stirring. Many of his contemporaries were at first uncomfortable with his boldness and unpredictability. But they were soon influenced enough to imitate Chopin's harmonics in their own work.

Love at Last

Chopin never married, although he was in love several times, and he did come close to marrying the young Maria Wodzinska, the daughter of a Polish count. The count would not allow it, though. No daughter of his was going to marry a piano player!

The woman he finally became close to was Amandine Aurore Dupin. She was a literary person, a novelist, who wrote under the pen name "George Sand." She not only took a man's name, she acquired male mannerisms as well, wearing masculine clothing and smoking cigars. She was liberated long before most women, refusing to let anyone place her in a category not of her own making.

Chopin was fascinated by her. At first she repelled him. Besides her smelly cigars, she wasn't very attractive to look at, and his fastidiousness and desire to be surrounded by beautiful things left no room for someone like George Sand. But her fine intellect and literary abilities appealed to his own artistic sensitivity. They became close friends, and would maintain a relationship for nine years.

In 1838 Chopin and George Sand went to the island of Majorca in the Mediterranean. They hoped to have a nice vacation, but it turned out to be a shattering experience. Chopin came down with a bad case of bronchitis. The townspeople, thinking he had infectious tuberculosis, forced the artists to abandon their comfortable villa and leave town.

They were able to find shelter in a monastery, but the damp and musty environment there made Chopin's bronchitis grow serious. A high fever brought on hemorrhages and hallucinations, and what started out as a simple cold almost killed him. George Sand brought him back to France where he eventually recovered, although never fully. Almost as if the Majorcans had wished it upon him, he did get tuberculosis and indeed would die from it.

A Dread Disease

The disease that Chopin suffered with took the lives of many artists of this period. In England, the young poet who could do with words what Chopin accomplished at the piano, was destined to live a very short life. John Keats (1795-1821) studied to be a doctor, not a poet. He earned his degree but decided against going into medicine. He wanted to be a poet and, at the age of twenty-one, devoted himself entirely to his art. He did not know he had only five years left to live. Keats' mother and brother died of tuberculosis, and he had caught it from them.

In those five years that he wrote poetry, Keats composed some of the most beautiful poems in the English language. His inspiration was beauty as expressed in the lines: " 'Beauty is truth, truth beauty,'— that is all/Ye know on earth, and all ye need to know."

To capture that beauty in words Keats used the technique of synaestheticism—evoking several senses at once. His poetry is filled with sounds and colors and even fragrances. As an example, here is the first stanza of his *Ode to Autumn:*

> Season of mists and mellow fruitfulness,
> Close bosom-friend of the maturing sun;
> Conspiring with him how to load and bless
> With fruit the vines that round the thatch-eaves run;
> To bend with apples the moss'd cottage-trees,
> And fill all fruit with ripeness to the core;
> To swell the gourd, and plump the hazel shells
> With a sweet kernel; to set budding more,
> And still more, later flowers for the bees,
> Until they think warm days will never cease.

Keats' poetry was also concerned with the artist's alienation from society, the intense artistic individualism that brought so much suffering and melancholy. Unlike Chopin and some of his other fellow artists, Keats failed to achieve any success while he was alive. More than most, he was to feel isolation and suffer from romantic melancholy. He died in obscurity, appreciated only by a few farsighted people like the poet Shelley. "I will compose my own epitaph," the dying Keats said to a friend. "Here lies one whose name was writ in water." But he was wrong, time has not, and will not, wash away his name.

Character Pieces

Composers made their own synaesthetics; mainly by creating new musical forms and sounds. Piano music was especially expanded during this time under the heading of Character Pieces. Each piece had its own mood and style, such as Fantasy, Impromptu, Etude. An entire list of character pieces would include the *Moments Musical* of Schubert, Beethoven's *Bagatelle,* Mendelssohn's *Songs Without Words* and Schumann's *Scenes from Childhood.* Schumann also linked together several different types of character pieces to form larger, more complex works like *Carnival* and *Papillons.*

Many of Chopin's finest works, his nocturnes, preludes, fantasies, and ballades, fit under this category. His nocturnes are quite in keeping with their name—dreamy music of the night, romantic and mysterious, and perfect for moonlit evenings. Chopin did not originate this form. In 1832 he heard the Irish composer John Field play some nocturnes, and he was inspired by Field's beautiful pieces to write some of his own.

Most of Chopin's nocturnes are characteristic of the romantic composer, with the tender yearning and sentimentality that we associate with them. At least one of Chopin's nocturnes, however, was intended as a "haunting" melody. The *Nocturne in G Minor,* inspired by a performance of Shakespeare's play *Hamlet,* is a good example. "The music," said Chopin, "describes a hushed night in Venice, a night that hides the movement of silent murderers, who slip the dead bodies of their victims into the sea." Haunting, indeed.

A character piece Chopin developed was the prelude. Preludes were usually associated with operas or stage plays, or were placed at the beginning of larger musical works like fugues or suites. Chopin enjoyed the miniature quality of the prelude and made them into a separate piano form. His preludes (he composed twenty-six of them) are usually short, and each one evokes a different mood. The "Raindrop" Prelude is probably his most famous. The rhythm, tapped out first by the left hand and then by the right, sounds very much like falling raindrops. The "Raindrop" Prelude takes about five minutes to play. In comparison, the extremely brief *Prelude in A Major* requires less than a minute to perform, but it is an especially penetrating minute, with its dance-like and nostalgic melody.

Chopin helped make the fantasy a character piece. The fantasy lets the composer develop the music slowly and completely according to his own mood. Chopin's *Fantaisie-Impromptu in C-sharp Minor* is his best known, having been turned into the popular song "I'm Always Chasing Rainbows." His *Fantaisie in F Minor,* however, is considered by critics to be his best effort in this form.

At one time in Chopin's career, he thought of becoming an actor. During his relationship with George Sand, when they and their friends entertained each other with theatrical performances, he was noted for his excellent acting abilities.

His ballades, a musical form longer than the others and more improvisational in character, allowed him to reveal his dramatic and poetic side. Like the program music Liszt was composing, Chopin's ballades were based on stories, although you do not need to know the story to appreciate the music. His first ballade was inspired by Maria, the daughter of the count who refused to let them marry. It was based on a story about valiant Christian knights fighting against pagan warriors, and allowed Chopin to release the conflicting passions he felt about the situation with Maria.

The most beautiful of the ballades, the fourth one, *Ballade in F Minor*, was not composed with any particular story in mind. Chopin simply let his imagination loose and, as a result, created some of his most outstanding melodies and harmonies that enchant the listener.

Some critics say that Chopin composed character pieces because he did not have the ability to write long works or to sustain inspiration over several movements. His sonatas, for instance, are not like Beethoven's: they are not developed so that each of the four movements represent an integral part of the whole. Chopin's sonatas are more like four separate works placed together under one title, a collection of four character pieces called sonatas.

Chopin's most famous composition in this form is the *Sonata in B-flat Minor.* This sonata does depart from the standard sonata form of Mozart and Beethoven. It contains many emotions, sorrow and despair, rage and demoniac frenzy. Anton Rubinstein, a great pianist, said it was like "howling winds of night sweeping over churchyard graves."

This is the sonata with the famous funeral march. The other three movements, while they can be listened to as separate pieces, nevertheless do contain an element of torment and death that unites all four movements. Chopin did not simply link together "four of his maddest children," as his friend Robert Schumann wrote.

Teaching a Queen

Chopin never fully regained his strength after Majorca. After 1841 his health began to get progressively worse. He could have accepted that, his spirit was still strong, and he continued to work. But George Sand was growing tired of him, and the next few years were unhappy ones, filled with domestic quarrels. Chopin had become strongly and irrevocably attached to her, and the impending breakup made him nervous and irritable.

In 1846 George Sand represented Chopin as one of the characters in her novel *Lucrezia Floriani*. It was not a flattering portrayal. She depicted him as a sickly aesthete, a person so wrapped up in his own creativeness that he could not communicate with his loved ones. Shortly after the publication of this novel, Chopin and Sand parted. "The end of this relationship," he told his friend Liszt, "means the end of my life. I do not think I can go on without her."

He was persuaded to try though, and he did try. In one last effort he traveled to England and Scotland, hoping to revive his interest in life and, hopefully, recoup his health. It wasn't difficult convincing the ill Chopin to visit London, it was 1848 and a revolution was raging in France.

In London he gave a number of small concerts and even some private piano lessons at the rate of one gold guinea a lesson. As the story goes, Queen Victoria, an amateur pianist, traveled incognito to Chopin's apartment to take lessons from him. He also met Charles Dickens, Thomas Carlyle, and Sir Walter Scott while in the British capital.

The Revolution of 1848 gave Chopin hope that Poland would become a separate nation again. His last public appearance, which took place in London, was a benefit for the Polish exiles, a charity that Chopin had contributed his time and talent to for almost twenty years.

Return to Poland

The trip to London only served to hasten the end. Chopin was very ill with consumption and knew that he was going to die. He returned to Paris. He could no longer teach or compose. His friends contributed to his upkeep. Relatives came from his beloved Poland to take care of him. Over the course of an entire year he weakened, steadily heading for death.

While very ill, he gave orders that his unfinished manuscripts be burned. He had always been a perfectionist about his art; he was determined that only his very best compositions would be available when he was gone.

On October 17, 1849, at twelve Place Vendome in Paris, a small second-story apartment away from the heart of the city, Frederic Chopin died. He was only thirty-nine years old. He had two last wishes which were carried out. The silver urn that his teacher had given him long ago, the one with the handful of Polish earth inside, was buried with Chopin's body in the Pere Lachaise cemetery in Paris. But his heart was removed from the body first—at his specific request—and carried back to Poland by his sister Louise. And there, in the country he so loved, his heart was laid to rest.

Postscript

Chopin is known as the Master of the Miniature. While most of the great composers wrote works for the piano, only Chopin devoted his entire attention to that instrument. Even his two concertos star the piano.

Unlike his contemporaries, Chopin did not have the desire to create large architectonic works. He was more than content to work with shorter forms, and he was not limited by composing in this fashion. As Rubinstein remarked: "He was so versatile. He could be tragic, romantic, lyric, heroic, fantastic, dramatic, sweet, soulful, dreamy, brilliant, grand, and simple—all with the piano."

Because of his remarkable versatility with this instrument, and the high standards he set in creating his music, Chopin has the distinction today of having more of his music performed, percentage-wise, than any other major composer. If he was "great in small forms," then it was a very large greatness.

Small forms or not, Chopin's contribution to the romantic movement was great. His individualism led him to develop a style of his own, expanding the melodic line of music while "thickening" the harmonic line with chromatic color; his nationalism brought the rhythms and melodies of Polish songs into the mainstream of European music; and even his sufferings—from ill health and unhappy love affairs—accounted for the strain of melancholy and longing in his work that marks the romantic temperament.

Study Activities

1. Prepare a written report on the history of keyboard instruments. What different types are there? When were they first invented, and what composers or performers are most often associated with them? This report should include accordions and any other wind or reed instruments that have keyboards.

2. Define each of the following terms, and give examples of how they are used.

rubato	arpeggio
nocturne	polonaise
chromatic	etude

3. George Sand wrote a novel, *Lucrezia Floriani,* about her relationship with Chopin. As a three-way project, read the book and give a report on it to your French, literature, and music classes.

4. Rewrite this C Major scale to make it a chromatic scale.

5. In the nineteenth century and part of the twentieth, France was the world leader in cultural matters. All other countries took their lead from France. Today America wields the greatest influence in cultural matters, and not only in the exportation of hamburger stands and Coca-cola. Discuss the many areas of cultural influence America now has. In what ways do other countries influence us?

III

Felix Mendelssohn:
The Gift of Song

Felix Mendelssohn was born one year before Chopin in Hamburg, Germany in 1809. He belonged to a prominent family. His father was a wealthy banker, and his mother was a highly educated and gifted artist. His grandfather, a renowned philosopher, was known as the German Plato.

There was no question about young Felix's own education. He received the best. When he exhibited the musical and artistic talents that he had inherited from his mother, he was immediately encouraged to develop them.

Mendelssohn, like Chopin and Mozart, was introduced to the piano by his older sister. Fanny Mendelssohn was a very lovely and talented person. She and Felix were exceptional in their early ability to grasp the fundamentals of music. When they were ready for serious lessons, their mother began instructing them. Later she obtained the finest teachers in Germany once they had advanced beyond her.

Felix's development at the piano was phenomenal. He outgrew his teachers as fast as his parents could replace them. Soon he turned his talents toward composing. The best teachers of composition were sought; the family settled on Karl Zelter, the director of the music academy. He was engaged to teach Mendelssohn musical theory.

The boy was so earnest about his studies that by the time he was twelve years old he had composed a number of practice symphonies. Just two years later he completed two one-act operas, some sonatas, and string quartets. There was nothing more any of his music teachers could show him that he did not already know. In fact, he left every one of them behind, his performances and compositions outdoing anything they could accomplish.

Mendelssohn

David and Saul

The greatest poet Germany ever produced was Johann Wolfgang von Goethe. His life spanned a large period of time, from 1749 to 1832, a total of eighty-three years. As a young man, he heard the child Mozart perform. In his old age, the child Mendelssohn was brought to him. "Another Mozart," Goethe said, and the two became fast friends. "Like Saul in the Bible, who had David to play and sing to him, I have you," Goethe told the young pianist.

It was fitting that Goethe was comforted in his old age by the most melodic of the young romantic composers. After all, it was Goethe's early work that helped ignite the romantic spirit. Throughout the nineteenth century composers turned to his poetry as the source of their inspiration. His famous novel, *The Sufferings of Young Werther,* a story about a tragic love affair, was turned into an opera by Massenet. The third act with its impassioned arias and the duet in which Werther is telling Charlotte of his love, only to be rejected by her, takes its place among the most beautiful and moving acts in opera.

Goethe's long dramatic poem *Faust* was also a favorite of the romantics, and was set to music by several composers in several different forms. Liszt's *Mephisto Waltz* is a demoniac piano rendition; Boito's opera *Mefistofele* and Gounod's *Faust* are based on Goethe's text; and Berlioz's *The Damnation of Faust,* a symphonic representation of the story, are just a few examples of Goethe's influence on the musical world.

By the time he died in 1832, Goethe had the pleasure of seeing his "David" successfully established in the music world.

The Conversion

Mendelssohn had many friends when he was young. He was a precocious and pleasant person, and everybody liked him. His parents, wanting to pave the way for him, brought him into contact with as many artists and influential people as they could, and a number of these people, like Goethe, remained his friends through life.

The Mendelssohns were famous for their entertaining. They lived in a grand house on a large estate and had all their friends over for weekly concerts and parties. Felix would play the works of Beethoven, Bach, and Mozart on the piano, and he would give concerts of his own compositions. There were also stage plays and musical dramas conducted by the young musician.

The Mendelssohns were devoted to their son. They knew he could become a great musician. But there was one thing in his path: his religion. The Mendelssohns were Jewish. Although a Jewish person might advance as far as his energy and intellect could take him in some fields, in other fields he was limited. To keep his son from bumping into a wall of prejudice, Abraham Mendelssohn, after consulting with his wife Leah, decided to convert to Protestantism and have his sons and daughters baptized. It was a difficult decision, cutting their ties with their Jewish tradition. But they all had faith in Felix, faith that he would begin a whole new tradition for all of them with his creative genius.

A Midsummer Night

Mendelssohn was only seventeen years old when he composed his famous *Overture* to *A Midsummer Night's Dream.* It was originally intended to be played by two pianos. His sister accompanied him on the family's second piano. It received such praise that Mendelssohn was persuaded to orchestrate it. Within a few months he was directing the Stettin orchestra in the first performance of the completed overture.

As program music, this overture perfectly captures the mood of Shakespeare's play. The fluttering violins in the beginning and end clearly portray the fairies, the hunting horns of Theseus are sounded, and even a suggestion of a donkey's braying can be heard.

The orchestral coloring in this piece brought instant acclaim to Mendelssohn. No other composer at the age of seventeen, not even Mozart, had shown such originality. The overture is introduced by the woodwinds. The fluttering violins take over until the orchestra suddenly bursts out in force. The horns and strings then present a short but lyrical theme, and the overture moves on in ever-increasing beauty, becoming a study in dynamics as well as tone color.

Mendelssohn composed the overture after having read Shakespeare's play. It was a natural response, and he did not plan to go any further with it. But sixteen years later, the King of Prussia, after hearing the overture, commissioned Mendelssohn to compose music for the entire play. Mendelssohn was happy to oblige. He composed twelve other pieces, including the *Scherzo* for the elfin Puck, the beautiful *Nocturne* for Acts Three and Four where the lovers have fallen asleep in the woods, and a number of dances and songs. The overture, scherzo, and nocturne are often excerpted for concert performances, and one other number is played quite often. In this series of incidental music can be found one of the world's favorite songs: Mendelssohn's *Wedding March,* a melody as indispensable at weddings as the minister. The march introduces Act Five of the play, where the triple wedding of Hermis and Lysander, Helena and Demetrius, and Hippolyta and Theseus takes place. The march heard at modern weddings is usually abbreviated. The fully orchestrated version as originally composed is far more exciting and entrancing.

The Bach Revival

Mendelssohn was not only gifted musically, he also was an excellent artist, learning drawing from his mother. He was constantly creating things, music and paintings, that were being admired. To top it off, he was an extremely handsome person, both as a child and an adult. Yet despite all the attention and praise he received, he managed to keep a good sense of balance about himself. He was not conceited or self-centered. In fact, he was more eager to give praise to others than to receive it. One of his most admirable actions in this regard was his dedication to the works of Johann Sebastian Bach.

Mendelssohn's mother was an admirer of Bach's music when hardly anyone other than professional musicians had even heard of the Leipzig composer. She and her husband collected Bach manuscripts, and passed on their enthusiasm for Bach and baroque art to their son.

In Berlin in 1829, after forming his own chorus and then convincing his friend Zelter to let the Music Academy work with him, Mendelssohn conducted Bach's *Passion According to St. Matthew.* This was the first public performance of one of Bach's major works since his death. Eighty years had gone by since the general public had last heard Bach, but after Mendelssohn's performance of the *Passion* there was a genuine Bach revival. Almost single-handedly, Mendelssohn rescued Bach from obscurity.

Bible Stories

Mendelssohn's interest in Bach's oratorios led him to write his own choral music. For some time he had been nursing an idea about a story in the Old Testament. "It will be about the prophet Elijah," he told the Rev. Schubring, who would write the text for him. "But we have to keep the large and long choral pieces from becoming boring. So concentrate on the dramatic elements. I want the singers to feel their parts, like actors."

The story of Elijah lends itself easily to drama. Elijah was a prophet in Israel 900 years before the birth of Christ. Israel was led by King Ahab and Queen Jezebel. The royal couple worshipped Baal, the Phoenician god. Elijah tried to warn them of their folly but they wouldn't listen. So a terrible drought came and devastated the land for three years.

Elijah warned the king and queen again. In a demonstration of fire, he managed to convince the people to turn against the pagan priests. Hundreds of the priests were seized and taken by Elijah into a valley near Kishon and slaughtered.

Queen Jezebel was not to be convinced. She sent men after Elijah to slay him, and he had to flee for his life. He prevailed, however, with the help of the God of Israel. King Ahab lost his throne. And Jezebel? "Eaten by the dogs," decreed God. And so she was.

At the end of his life, a chariot of fire was sent for Elijah to take him up "by a whirlwind" into heaven.

The music in *Elijah* is very stirring. It is highly melodic and intensely dramatic and is equally effective in a theater or a church. When the oratorio was performed for the first time (in Birmingham, England in 1846), Mendelssohn was given the greatest ovation of his life—which is saying a lot when you consider that by then he was already the most idolized composer in Europe.

The Light Touch

Mendelssohn's love of Bach steeped him strongly in tradition, but not only in the tradition of the baroque era. He had a great deal in common with Mozart and Schubert: he had the temperament of a romantic, the desire to make his music free and flowing, but he was devoted to classical forms, the sonatas and symphonies, as well as to the preclassical forms like the fugue. He was not an innovator in form and technique like the other romantics, preferring rather to use the forms of the past.

Yet he did make some changes. One of his early chamber works, the *Octet in E-flat Major,* is scored for eight instruments, a unique number. And this was done when Mendelssohn was only sixteen years old. Another innovation appears in his third symphony: Mendelssohn wanted all four movements played without any pauses between them.

Mendelssohn's music has often been called cultured and refined in the manner of the classicists; he did not display his inner feelings with the same intensity as the other romantics. And to a large extent this is true. Even in his personal life he liked to keep cool and collected, subduing his tensions and emotions. A letter to his mother concerning his coming marriage indicates his restrained nature. "I will be calm and collected and go through this affair with the coolness I have always managed to show when taking an important step in life."

Mendelssohn's music matches his nature perfectly. He was not like the stormy Beethoven or profound Brahms. He had a wonderfully happy childhood, a carefree adolescence, and an astonishing degree of success as an adult; so it is strange for the critics to seek the same passionate outcries in his work that they find in the other romantics. The key to romantic expression is individualism, and Mendelssohn's music certainly conveys that. The lyrical quality of his melodies, the unabrasive harmonies and gay orchestral scoring are all indicative of the man himself. His work *does* express his feelings, and it is a pleasant change in this period to come across a perfectly happy man. The unhappy love affairs of Chopin, the tortured mind of Schumann, the religious doubts of Liszt, the vitriolic hates of Wagner, or the sexual inadequacies of Tchaikovsky, play no part in Mendelssohn's life. His was the light touch, yet also the lasting touch. His ability to conceive so many beautiful and memorable melodies has always kept Mendelssohn in a class by himself.

Fingal's Cave

Mendelssohn's music quickly spread from Germany and was soon being played all over Europe. He received invitations from the major cities to conduct concerts, and he went on an extensive tour, carrying his music and conductor's baton (he was the first to use one) with him.

Mendelssohn enjoyed traveling. Of all the cities he visited, London pleased him the most. And he pleased the Londoners; they thoroughly enjoyed his music. Their appreciation for his work was so evident that Mendelssohn was persuaded to give a number of premieres there. He eventually visited England on ten different occasions.

When he was twenty years old, he traveled to Scotland. He went to see Fingal's Cave, a scenic spot in the Hebrides Islands west of Scotland. When he saw the waves from the ocean washing in and out of the cavern's mouth, and the rays of the overhead sun glistening on the water and spraying bits of fairy light into the dark opening of the cavern, he knew that he would have to set this experience to music. It was a majestic scene, and the music it inspired, the *Hebrides Overture,* is equally captivating and majestic. The dynamic crescendos in the opening of the overture perfectly capture the effect of rolling waves. The melodies in this piece are considered by many to be the greatest he ever wrote. And there is no questioning the romantic quality of this work. The romantic modulations and overlapping orchestration directly affect the listener's emotions, involving him in the same excitement that Mendelssohn felt when he first saw the cave.

After listening to the *Hebrides,* which is one of the most sensuous pieces of music ever composed, it is hard to understand how Mendelssohn grew out of favor with the later romantics, who accused him of being too much of a classicist and not conveying enough romantic expression in his work.

The Travel Symphonies

Mendelssohn composed five major symphonies (seventeen, if you count the twelve symphonies he wrote as a boy when first learning composition). His two most famous symphonies were inspired by his travels, his *Symphony No. 3,* the "Scotch," and *No. 4,* the "Italian." All his symphonies, but especially these two, show his dual nature, the romantic spirit poured forth into classical forms.

The first movement of the "Scotch" Symphony opens with a melancholy but moving song, the strings, flutes, and clarinets trying to capture the misty landscape of Scotland. There are no special rhythms or songs in this movement that are unique to Scotland. It is in the second movement that Mendelssohn employs a perky Scottish dance, where the clarinets and strings have a chance to show off their lighter side, making this symphony a contrast in moods. More Scottish melodies and rhythms appear in the last movement, which repeats the melancholy attitude of the first movement, yet ends in a lively extended coda.

Although Mendelssohn began writing the "Scotch" Symphony within two years after his visit to Scotland, he postponed completing it until 1842, thirteen years later. Instead he worked on his "Italian" Symphony.

He went to Italy after being in Scotland and was charmed by the brightness of that country. It presented quite a contrast to the overcast skies of England and Scotland. Unlike the "Scotch" Symphony, which uses various Scottish melodies in an attempt to capture the changing moods and landscapes of Scotland, the "Italian" Symphony, while also employing local rhythms, is consistent in tone. "It is the merriest piece I have yet composed," Mendelssohn wrote to his sister. "It captures the charm and liveliness of this wonderful country." Light and gay melodies pervade the entire work. Even the second movement, which is slower and subdued in tone, serves to highlight the overall vivacity of the symphony.

Better Than Words

Mendelssohn's creativeness and originality is best seen in his *Songs Without Words,* piano pieces that try to capture the quality of a vocal song without using words. Mendelssohn believed that, in comparison to music, words were indefinite and ambiguous, and were not nearly as effective as they might be. He was asked why he didn't supply words to this beautiful series of piano pieces. In a letter to his friend, Marc Souchay, he stated his views:

> There is so much talk about music, and yet so little is said. For my part, I believe that words do not suffice for such a purpose, and if I found they did I would finally have nothing more to do with music. People often complain that music is too ambiguous, that what they should be thinking as they hear it is unclear, whereas everyone understands words. With me it is exactly the reverse. Words are so ambiguous, so vague, so easily misunderstood in comparison to genuine music which fills the soul with a thousand things better than words. The thoughts which are expressed to me by music are not too indefinite to be put into words, but on the contrary, too definite. And so I find in every

effort to express such thoughts in words that something is always lacking. If you ask me what I was thinking of when I wrote a certain song, I would say: just the song as it stands. And if I happen to have had certain words in mind for one or another of these songs, I would never want to tell them to anyone, because the same words seldom mean the same things to different people. Only the song can say the same thing, can arouse the same feelings in one person as in another, a feeling which is not expressed, however, by the same words.

The main point of the letter is that people should not be trying to say what music is—but *feeling* it. It's like being outdoors on a beautiful spring day. Trying to capture that day in words is futile. Remember how wonderful a fresh day in spring *feels?* There is the clean cool air, the warming rays of the sun, the fresh smell of grass, the newly budding trees, the early spring flowers just beginning to bloom, the whole intense feeling of rebirth and happiness that one experiences just being outside. How can all these feelings— the sense of smell, hearing, sight, and touch—ever be equalled by words?

Building an Institution

While on his conducting tours, Mendelssohn came into contact with all the great composers of his time, including Chopin and Liszt in Paris. He and his wife (he married Cecile Jeanrenaud in 1837) were also friends with Robert and Clara Schumann in Leipzig.

Before his marriage, Mendelssohn had been the music director of the city of Düsseldorf. He took the post to gain experience as a professional director, but he did not like the work—at least not with the Düsseldorf musicians. Mendelssohn set rather high standards and received more resistance from the musicians than results. After six months he left the city in disgust. "I gladly leave the Düsseldorfers to their own mediocrity," he said.

He soon became the director of the Leipzig orchestra. From 1835 through 1840 Mendelssohn directed this orchestra with great energy and skill. These musicians were happy to accept his advice for improving their performances. Before he left Leipzig to take charge of the construction and planning of the Berlin Academy of Arts, the Leipzig Gewandhaus Orchestra was considered one of the best in the world, and Mendelssohn's reputation as director and conductor was excelled by no one.

Mendelssohn did not like Berlin. He missed Leipzig. He was happy when the Berlin Academy of Arts did not go beyond the drawing board stage. He accepted the post as chapelmaster to the Prussian king, but only on the condition that he could perform his duties in Leipzig.

Back in Leipzig he got together with the King of Saxony to discuss a matter that had been on his mind for some time. Now that Berlin was not going to have their Academy, this was the best time to build a conservatory of music in Leipzig. "We can make Leipzig a cultural center," the composer insisted. The king agreed, but only if Mendelssohn would take complete charge.

In April of 1843 the Leipzig Conservatory of Music was officially opened, and Mendelssohn proved himself a great administrator. He and Schumann conducted classes in piano and composition; his friend Ferdinand David was the violin professor; and the school soon became one of the most prestigious in Germany.

The Gypsy Bow

It was for his friend, Ferdinand David, that Mendelssohn composed his famous *Violin Concerto in E Minor.* There are only a handful of violin concertos that are considered great, those by Mozart, Beethoven, Brahms, and Tchaikovsky, and Mendelssohn's is among them. His is also the one most performed today.

In the violin concerto, as in this *Third Symphony*, Mendelssohn didn't want any pauses between the movements. He wanted to maintain the impetus once the music started, and he wanted a very fast start. The violin comes in almost immediately in the concerto, preceded only by a few notes from the orchestra. With the solo violin, one of the most impassioned gypsy melodies is heard. Here are a few bars of that melody:

The concerto, like all of Mendelssohn's music, was an instant success. He seemed to know instinctively just what the public wanted, and he was always able to provide it without compromising any of his artistic aims.

The Blood Tie

Throughout the 1840s, Mendelssohn was conducting the Gewandhaus Orchestra in Leipzig, composing his *Elijah* oratorio and other works, traveling back and forth to England and other countries, and making numerous public appearances, not to mention establishing the Leipzig Conservatory. He was overworking himself and should have taken a rest. But music kept running through his head and he felt compelled to get it all written down. "This concerto," he wrote to David, "keeps racing through my mind. It gives me no peace."

So he kept up his frenzied activity, composing, conducting, teaching, traveling. Throughout all this, he managed to keep close contact with his family. His wife and sisters tried to get him to go at a slower pace, but he just couldn't.

In May 1847, after traveling from Leipzig to London, then on to Birmingham, Manchester, and finally to Frankfort, Mendelssohn did decide to take a vacation. He was tired and irritable and finally listened to his family. But then someone brought him terrible news. On May 14th in Berlin, his sister Fanny, who had been his closest friend since childhood, had suffered a stroke and died. The news was so shocking that it caused Mendelssohn, exhausted from so much hard work, to faint. A blood vessel ruptured in his head, and he, too, had a stroke. Although he managed to recover, within six months he had another stroke and on November 4, 1847, at the age of thirty-eight, Felix Mendelssohn died.

The Essential Link

Because of his semiaristocratic upbringing, where a respect for tradition played an important role, Mendelssohn was never completely a romantic. He was not Byronic in nature, moody, or temperamental. He purposely toned down the subjective element of his work, emulating Mozart rather than Beethoven; and he was content to follow the baroque and classical composers as far as musical forms were concerned.

Despite his conservatism; Mendelssohn was the most popular of all the early romantic composers, eclipsing Chopin, Schumann, Berlioz, and even Franz Liszt, in the public's esteem. There was a good reason for this. In a time of great and rapid changes, when the romantic rebel seemed to be challenging everything, Mendelssohn's was a stabilizing influence, linking the new with the old. By uniting the present forms and sounds with those of the past, he made the future seem a little less uncertain.

Mendelssohn reaffirmed for the other romantic composers the continuing value and usefulness of traditional forms. By demonstrating how they could be reshaped and revitalized, Mendelssohn contributed greatly to the continuity of music history.

Study Activities

1. Our two most popular songs that celebrate weddings songs come from the romantic period, from Mendelssohn's *Midsummer Night's Dream* and Wagner's *Lohengrin*. In both cases they are marches. Why a march? What other rhythm might be suitable for the occasion? Can you compose a melody that you think would sound nice at a wedding?

2. Next to each word in the following list place the letter C, R, or T, depending on whether it describes classic, romantic, or twentieth century music. If you think a word might describe more than one style, use a combination of letters.

Sonata-allegro	Chromaticism	Art song
Subjectivism	Chamber music	Tone poem
Contrast	Atonality	Concerto

3. Mendelssohn wrote: "Music is more definite than words." It is true that many words are ambiguous. Compile a list of ten words that have different meanings for different people, and state what those meanings are. Example: "communism" (a political system that represses individual freedom; a theory calling for community ownership of property and national production, with each member getting a fair share). Can you see how misunderstandings of such important words can cause international problems?

4. The romantic poets had a keen interest in nature. But they all had different perceptions of how nature and man interact. Read Wordsworth's *Michael,* Coleridge's *Rime of the Ancient Mariner,* Shelley's *Ode to the West Wind,* and Keats' *To Autumn* and discuss the varying presentations of man and nature in these poems.

IV

Robert Schumann:
Tortured Genius

What can be more frustrating than being forced into a career you don't really want? That was Robert Schumann's problem.

At first, his parents were pleased with his childhood interests. His father, an author and publisher, had an extensive library; and when they saw their son in it every day avidly reading one book after another, it fit quite well into their plans for him. They expected him to become a lawyer.

So Schumann was not as lucky as Chopin and Mendelssohn. When he displayed a talent for music at an early age, he was not encouraged. His father let him learn the piano and a little music theory, but his mother was not at all pleased by it. Later, when his father died, Schumann received no encouragement to continue his artistic studies.

Schumann's mother was determined that her son would become a lawyer. In order to please her, he attended law school, but his heart wasn't in it. Schumann went to the University of Leipzig to study law, but he was not a very good student. While in Leipzig, he spent most of his time at concerts. He went to the piano teacher Friedrich Wieck and began taking lessons from him.

His mother insisted he continue with his proper studies and managed to get him transferred to the beautiful University of Heidelberg. Even in Heidelberg, he spent the greatest part of the day playing the piano and composing, staying at the piano for as much as eight hours in one day. He also traveled to Italy to hear Paganini give a

Clara and Robert Schumann

violin concert, which only made him more determined to have a musical career of his own.

Finally, in November 1829, he decided for himself that he was not going to become a lawyer, no matter how much that decision disappointed his mother. He was nineteen years old and felt certain that he knew his own mind. He could feel within himself the overwhelming urge to be musical. He knew he could learn to play the piano as well as any of the virtuosos he had come in contact with. "Within six years," he wrote to his mother, trying desperately to convince her, "I know I will be a challenge for any of them." He was going to be a musician. Finally, with his mother's reluctant consent, Schumann returned to Leipzig and again took lessons from Wieck.

Too Much Haste

Schumann could not suppress the frustration he felt at having wasted so many years at law, years that could have gone into perfecting his real talent. He wanted to make up for that lost time, so he studied the piano with a maniac's devotion, making Wieck show him every technique possible within the shortest space of time.

"I could go mad with all this music in my head, waking me in the middle of the night, calling me to the piano." Schumann had a very hypersensitive nature, and having been frustrated for so many years only made it more so.

Wieck tried to convince his impetuous student to be more patient: "Eile mit weile," he would tell him, "hurry. . .but take your time." But Schumann felt that he had to make up for lost time. In order to speed things up, he did constant finger exercises. Then he foolishly went a step further. "I must make all my fingers independent of each other," he said. And to achieve this impossible effect, he went about devising a strap for his ring finger, to keep it from moving when the middle finger was bent. He wore the device for some time, disregarding the pain in his hand, as he sat at the piano for hours and played. When he finally removed the straps from his ring finger, he found to his despair that it would no longer work. Without realizing what he was doing, this budding virtuoso, who could have been a great pianist, had crippled his right hand.

You can imagine what torture he must have gone through. First disbelief: surely the finger would be normal again in a few hours; then despair when he fully understood what he had done; then rage, at himself for his stupid haste, and at his mother and the world for having "conspired" against him.

It was fortunate for Schumann's sanity that he had higher goals than just performing music. He wanted to compose music, and a paralyzed finger couldn't stop him from doing that. So he struggled on. He went to Heinrich Dorn to learn music theory. For the next three years, between 1830 and 1833, he immersed himself in the problems of composing, working on a symphony and on several character pieces for the piano.

Musical Anagrams

Schumann's unbounded energy kept him going, and his youth kept him hopeful. He met a young woman in Mannheim, named Pauline Abegg, who helped relieve his depression. He composed a theme with the musical notes A B E G G and then created several variations of it. Known as the *Abegg Variations,* it is still performed at recitals today.

Schumann was fond of such musical games, taking the letters of names and transposing them into musical notes. His famous *Carnaval,* a series of brief piano pieces depicting the characters in a carnival, also displays his penchant for musical anagrams. The subtitle of this work is "Tiny Scenes on Four Notes." The notes are A S C H, after the German town of Asch where another of his girlfriends lived. In German, "S" is written out as "Es," which is the musical notation for E-flat; and the German "H," musically speaking, is our B-natural. The fact that these letters also appeared in Schumann's own name intrigued him even more.

Schumann used these letters to devise three separate themes, and then he used these themes with variations to represent the different figures in a carnival. There are no less than twenty-one "Tiny Scenes" in *Carnaval,* each one stemming from those four notes.

Another popular series of piano pieces is Schumann's *Kinderscenen, Scenes from Childhood.* There are thirteen separate songs in this set. One of Schumann's best known melodies, "Dreaming," is from *Kinderscenen.*

Schumann wanted to bring about a change in musical forms. While he would eventually compose sonatas and symphonies, he insisted that his loosely-knit works, like *Carnaval* and *Kinderscenen,* had a form that was best suited for their individual contents. Perhaps more than any other romantic composer, Schumann's works have this entirely personal element. "My compositions are hard to understand because they are associated with my own interests; anything that happens around me impresses me and compels me to express it in music. Each work of art has its own meaning," he insisted, "and its own special form." To place all his inspiration in only the forms that existed meant to deny the uniqueness of his own ideas. If they were conceived as sonatas, then he would write them in sonata form. But if they were conceived as a series of pictures, brief musical vignettes, he would devise a new form, if necessary, to best exhibit them. His insistence in this matter, to shape each work to fit the originating impulse, however transitory or fleeting the idea, makes Schumann the forerunner of the impressionists, both in music and in art.

The Composer as Critic

Schumann's interest in composing went beyond his own work. He was greatly interested in the works of his contemporaries. In 1833 he established a musical society with several of his friends. Their purpose was to seek out new composers and introduce them to the public: and also to help the public distinguish between the great and the mundane among the established composers. They published a magazine called the *New Journal of Music* which Schumann edited.

During the ten years that he would be a music critic, Schumann would be among the first in Germany to sing the praises of Chopin, in his early essays, and of Brahms, in his last writings. He also had the courage to challenge the mastery of Rossini and Meyerbeer when everyone else was singing their praises. And taking the lead from Mendelssohn, he helped bring the music of Bach once again before the public, writing several essays about the baroque composer.

Schumann felt within himself two separate characters: a quiet and introspective one, and a quick-tempered passionate one. He named these conflicting moods Eusebius and Florestan and first represented them as characters in his *Carnaval.* He used these fictitious names to sign some of his articles written for the *New Journal* depending on his mood, whether he was attacking some mediocre talent or praising a great one. Writing essays for the magazine, when he was not composing his music, helped to keep him from becoming depressed, a mental condition that was seriously beginning to interfere with his daily activities.

The Manfred Influence

Schumann's mental health was never stable. He tried too much to "feel" life; he became overly sensitive to external stimuli. He would hear a beautiful melody and get so carried away that he would be in tears before he knew it; or he would read a novel and become so involved in the action that he often brought himself to the edge of madness. This mental intensity was in part brought on by his susceptibility to his readings in Byron and in Goethe, and in part inherited from his family. There was a degree of madness in the Schumann family. His father suffered from a nervous disorder and went insane before he died; and his sister, Emilia, was born a mental defective. She wound up killing herself.

Schumann tried to commit suicide, too. For a long time pressure had built up within him. First, there was his mother and her machinations to get him into the law profession; then there was the heartbreaking incident which paralyzed his finger; and finally, a feeling of self-doubt that he would ever become a great composer. No one seemed to understand his work, or to even want to try. In October 1833, Schumann reread Byron's poetic drama *Manfred.* Manfred, the hero of the play, is steeped in melancholy and isolation. Unable to discover the meaning of existence, he attempts to throw himself off a cliff. He is saved by a hunter who arrives in time to stop him. Shortly after reading this, Schumann decided to take similar action. Had it not been for some timely interference by an acquaintance, which kept Schumann from hurling himself out of a window, the young composer would have died at the age of twenty-three.

A Father's Love

Schumann seemed to be destined for bad luck. One of the hardest struggles was still facing him. He had fallen in love with Clara Wieck, the daughter of his piano teacher, and she loved him. But her father was dead set against their marriage. As a pupil, Robert Schumann was one thing, but as a son-in-law? The father would not have it. In his eyes Schumann was a loser: he spent years studying law but failed to become a lawyer; he worked madly studying the piano but failed to become a pianist; and now he was composing and not getting anywhere with that. Looking at it from Friedrich Wieck's angle, Schumann had nothing going for him. Besides Wieck had other plans for Clara. She was a gifted pianist, one of the few women virtuosos, and Wieck was going to see that she used her talents.

Despite the father's objections, the young couple became engaged. Wieck was so outraged that he began a vicious campaign against Schumann, spreading rumors that he was an alcoholic and didn't deserve the support and respect of honest people. He then arranged an extensive concert tour for Clara, and insisted she leave immediately. He, of course, went with her.

Whenever they could, the lovers would write each other letters, using mutual friends to insure their arrival. But during years of separation, they were able to see each other only on rare occasions. When they could meet face to face, rare and exhilarating moments for them, they would renew their pledge of love and their determination to be together.

They would have to wait four years, enduring all sorts of mean and petty tricks by the angry father, before they could get married. Even then, they had to go to court to get permission to marry without the father's consent. After months of distressing arguments during the court trial, Robert and Clara won. On September 12, 1840 they were married. It would be a long time before Friedrich Wieck would forgive his daughter.

The Sonnet of Love

There is an interesting historical parallel between the Schumanns' love affair and what happened to the poets Elizabeth Barrett and Robert Browning in England just four years later. Like Robert Schumann, Robert Browning could not find initial acceptance for his art. His poems were considered confusing, and it took him twenty years to get his contemporaries to accept him. He, too, was considered a "loser."

In 1844 he read some poetry by the very popular poetess Elizabeth Barrett. In one of her poems, there was a brief reference to him and his poetry—a *kind* reference. Browning was as surprised by it as he was grateful, and he immediately wrote her a long letter asking to see her and thank her in person. An impulsive man (here too he was like Schumann), he added a postscript insisting he had fallen in love with her through her poems.

It was Elizabeth's turn to be surprised. She was startled by the unexpected love letter. She was a sick woman, an invalid actually without any hope of walking. She had injured her spine when she was fifteen, while riding a horse. She wasn't used to such amorous attention. And though Browning persisted in his request to see her by sending dozens of follow-up letters, it was months before she would consent to let her admirer visit her.

Browning visited more than once. Seeing Elizabeth only deepened his feelings for her. It took him several months to convince Elizabeth that she too could love and contemplate a normal life and, perhaps, even recover from her invalidism. She was already beginning to be more active physically, thanks to his encouragement.

Browning soon confronted the same obstacle to his love as Schumann had: the father. Elizabeth and her father had a very close relationship, even then when Elizabeth was thirty-eight years old. They depended on each other for companionship. But when Browning came on the scene, Elizabeth no longer needed her father. She still loved him, of course, but her deepest love was now given to Robert Browning.

Elizabeth's father had strange ideas about his children. He had eleven in all and was determined to keep them all together. He became enraged whenever any of them spoke of marriage or of creating a separate life for themselves. In 1846, jealous of Browning's continuous attention to his daughter, he refused to let him visit the house. But when he told Elizabeth that he was going to move her out into the country where no one could find her, she rebelled. On September 12th, she managed to get out of the house, meet Browning, and marry him. They went to Italy, where Browning hoped the warm climate might help restore Elizabeth's health. And it did. She completely recovered under his care and love and was even able to have a child. She wrote for Browning her beautiful *Sonnets From the Portuguese,* a collection of poems celebrating their love. Of the forty-four sonnets in that volume, the forty-third is the best known:

> How do I love thee? Let me count the Ways.
> I love thee to the depth and breadth and height
> My soul can reach, when feeling out of sight
> For the ends of Being and ideal Grace.
> I love thee to the level of everyday's
> Most quiet need, by sun and candle-light.
> I love thee freely, as men strive for Right;
> I love thee purely, as they turn from Praise.
> I love thee with the passion put to use
> In my old griefs, and with my childhood's faith.
> I love thee with a love I seemed to lose
> With my lost saints,—I love thee with the breath,
> Smiles, tears, of all my life!—and, if God choose,
> I shall but love thee better after death.

This poem serves as an expression of love for both the Brownings and the Schumanns. Elizabeth died after sixteen years of a happy marriage, and Robert Browning cherished her memory for the next thirty years, never remarrying. And to complete the parallel, Robert Schumann would die after sixteen years of marriage, and Clara would cherish his memory for decades without ever remarrying. The nineteenth century is well named Romantic.

Musical Sonnets

Until he married Clara, Schumann composed mostly piano music. In the first year of their marriage, he experimented with vocal music, setting poetry to music. He had long been an admirer of Franz Schubert's art songs; influenced by Schubert and inspired by his new bride, Schumann composed more than 250 love songs of his own. For the text of his famous song cycle, *A Poet's Love,* which he dedicated to Clara, Schumann used the poetry of Heinrich Heine. It was a perfect match, the exquisite poems of Heine with the equally exquisite melodies of Schumann.

Like Schubert, Schumann was able to envision and compose just the right melody for the poems. And unlike anyone else, Schumann was able to make his music amplify the meaning of each poem. He ends the song, "In the Glorious Month of May," for instance, on a half cadence, which corresponds to the tone of questioning about love and death in the poem. He uses special harmonic effects, if the poem seems to require a thicker texture; and he reins in his lyricism, if the subject of the poem seems contrary to the usual melodic treatment, as in the poem, "I am not Angry."

More than anyone before him, Schumann made the piano and voice subtle partners. He also added lyrical preludes and postludes so that the piano could better complement the mood of the poetry.

Bigger Things

Schumann's interest in orchestral compositions came in 1841, mostly at the suggestion of Clara. She, along with Mendelssohn and some of their other friends, believed that Schumann would have a better chance at establishing a reputation if he worked on larger forms. Schumann agreed.

He preferred to keep his instrumentation simple. In this regard he was like the classicists—and influenced by Mendelssohn. He was not after dramatic effects like Berlioz, or huge architectonic structures like Brahms or Wagner.

Again, the influence of Schubert is present in Schumann's reliance on a succession of melodies to build up his symphonic works, rather than on one or two major themes which are then developed and recapitulated.

Schumann composed his first and third symphonies with a distinct idea in mind for each, although they are not programmatic. His *Symphony No. 1* tries to capture the freshness of spring. There is a generous use of horns and woodwinds throughout the composition, interspersed with beautiful melodies for the string section.

His *Symphony No. 2* again makes use of the trumpets, but to represent an entirely different mood, this time sad and melancholy. Beethoven enjoyed this method of making his symphonies a successive contrast of moods.

Schumann's *Third Symphony*, completed in 1850, is an attempt to musically depict Rhenish life. Instead of the usual four movements, Schumann composed five, interjecting ecclesiastical music between the third and concluding movement to capture the religious quality of the Rhenish folk.

His *Fourth Symphony*, in the key of D minor, is a study in unity. The four movements are so smoothly connected that it seems like one large movement with several sections. Again his melancholy side emerges when the oboes and cellos, with their rich deep voices, are played against a background of plucked strings. But the symphony ends on a lively, even joyous, note, emphasizing once more the strong contrast of moods that made up Schumann's nature.

His most important orchestral composition was started in the spring of 1841, when Schumann began composing his *Fantasie in A Minor,* a single movement work for piano and orchestra. It was finished by that summer, and in August, his wife played it with the Leipzig Orchestra. "It is a beautiful piece," she wrote in her diary, "and will definitely give pleasure to all who hear it."

But Schumann wasn't satisfied with it. After a publisher refused to accept it, Schumann decided to rework it into a more popular form. In Dresden four years later, he added an Intermezzo and Finale for it. Clara was very pleased. "I have always wanted a great bravura concerto by him," she wrote. And wherever she went on her concert tours, she performed what was now his *Piano Concerto in A Minor.*

The structure of his concerto is, of course, unique because it was begun as a fantasy. The first movement has a sense of improvisation, with its quick changes of tempo and tone. The third movement also includes a free fantasia section. And to underline his break from the classical concerto, Schumann dispensed with the customary pause between the second and third movements and blended them together. It was this concerto, and Clara's insistence on playing it on all her concert tours, that eventually convinced the critics and the public that Schumann was worth listening to.

The Hand of Friendship

Despite his problems in obtaining an audience for his own work, Schumann was still interested in introducing new composers to the public. It was through Schumann's understanding and generosity that the young Johannes Brahms was brought to public attention.

The young Brahms, who was quite taken with Schumann's compositions, stopped by one day to pay his idol a visit. Schumann asked him to play a few pieces for him. When he heard Brahms' music, he was enchanted. "You'll stay with us," he told the visitor. And the brief visit turned into a three month stay, beginning a friendship that would last until Schumann's death, and then afterward between Brahms and Clara for forty years.

During the three month visit, Schumann wrote an article for the *New Journal* praising Brahms' music; then he helped the twenty-three year old composer find a publisher. Clara included a number of Brahms' sonatas and other pieces for the piano in her repertory, playing both her husband's and the young Brahms' music at her recitals.

A number of years before he met Brahms, Schumann made yet another contribution to the history of music. He went to Vienna to visit the brother of Franz Schubert. He hoped to get some personal information for an article he was writing about Schubert. The brother showed Schumann a package of manuscripts that had been lying on a shelf in a closet since Schubert's death. Schumann eagerly looked through them, and, to his great surprise and joy, he found the *Symphony in C Major*. "This must be played," he told the brother, "it must be brought to the public." He arranged to have the manuscript published, and, in his article for the *New Journal,* he wrote about his discovery. "The greatest symphony since Beethoven," was his judgement. His friend Mendelssohn conducted the symphony in its first performance, a performance that might never have been given, had it not been for Schumann's appreciation of Franz Schubert's work.

In Clara's Shadow

Robert and Clara Schumann had a happy marriage, one that brought them eight children. They had numerous friends and were able, even with their many children, to travel about Europe advancing their music. Clara's playing sometimes brought in more money than Schumann's conducting, and that occasionally caused some unhappiness for Schumann. Schumann's wife was more famous than he. At one time, in Russia in 1844, a Russian nobleman came up to him and said: "Your wife plays beautifully. And you. . . are you musical too?"

Mendelssohn's invitation to Schumann to teach at the new Conservatory of Leipzig was one of the few recognitions of Schumann's musical abilities that he was to receive in his lifetime. It gave him a new sense of self-confidence, and he tried hard to fulfill his duties. But his mental stability was threatened by a nervous disorder.

The Schumanns moved to Dresden in 1844 for Robert's health. They stayed there for five years, Clara continuing to give occasional concerts and still managing to care for their many children, and Robert writing fugues in the manner of Bach and working on his *Symphony No. 2.* They met Richard Wagner in Dresden, whose operas were beginning to attract wide attention. Schumann admired Wagner's work and told him so; Wagner scarcely tolerated Schumann's.

To overcome some of their financial difficulties, Schumann accepted a post in Dusseldorf as director of the orchestra. But by that time, his mental health was deteriorating. He was not able to do a very good job and had to resign.

A Darker Shadow

Schumann's later problems were all mental; he suffered from long periods of depression; he thought he heard voices; and he even claimed that the spirits of Mozart and Bach visited him and gave him melodies.

It is easy to understand what was so deeply troubling him. Schumann was not appreciated in his own lifetime. He did not share in the happiness that Chopin, Mendelssohn, and most of the composers enjoyed, hearing their work performed to the applause of an enthusiastic audience. Though Mendelssohn tried to understand Schumann's work, only Franz Liszt, of all the romantics, thoroughly understood and appreciated him. But even Liszt seldom played Schumann's piano compositions at his many recitals.

In his lucid moments, Schumann knew he was going insane. "My music," he wrote, "is gone forever." In February of 1852, he again tried to commit suicide, this time by throwing himself off a bridge overlooking the Rhine river.

Robert Schumann spent the final two years of his life in an insane asylum, totally withdrawn from reality and further rejections of his work. He died in 1856, never realizing that his work was already becoming popular, and that his name would be linked with the other musical greats of his age.

Clara Wieck Schumann lived for another forty years, forever faithful to her husband's life work. After all her hard work to help her husband, she was able to see his fame, and hers, grow and take root in the history of music.

Guiding Principles

Schumann's romanticism is best seen in his personality. His was truly a Byronic temperament, moody, melancholy, and enshrouded in a cocoon. He isolated himself even from the woman he loved, to the extent that madness ensued.

He was also one of the most original composers of the early romantics. Like Mendelssohn he revered the masters of classicism and often housed his expressive music in their old forms. But his piano compositions had little precedent. He was Chopin's counterpart, developing the character piece and other miniature songs that overflowed with warm melodies, unique harmonies, and vibrant rhythms.

The romantic sense of individualism and the romantic interest in new approaches to life and art were Schumann's guiding principles. It is a great pity that the romantic intensity of feeling and emotionalism was so exaggerated in Schumann, leading to his breakdown and death.

Study Activities

1. Take four letters from your full name that coincide with the musical notes A through G (use a relative's name if necessary). Compose six simple tunes using those four notes as a base. You can use other notes with them, but each melody should obviously be "rooted" in your name.

2. G. Meyerbeer (1791-1864) and G. Rossini (1792-1868) both composed operas that were extremely popular during the first half of the romantic period. How many operas did each compose? What kind of operas were they (tragedy, comedy, melodrama, etc.)? Discuss, either in an oral report or in a written essay, at least one of their more popular operas (the story and the music) in detail.

3. Chopin and Schumann liked to compose character pieces for the piano, describing their thoughts and feeling about life in music. What would make good subjects for character pieces today? Make a list of ten, such as *Moon Journey*. A modern *Carnaval* might be titled *Disneyworld*.

4. Match the author or composer with his work:

Mendelssohn	*Scenes from Childhood*
Byron	*Portuguese Sonnets*
Schumann	*Symphony in C Major*
Browning	*Manfred*
Schubert	*Hebrides*

V

Hector Berlioz:
The Bad Boy of Music

Unlike most major composers, Berlioz could not play musical instruments. He played a little guitar, but even that not very well.

Berlioz did not feel jealous of those who could perform brilliantly on pianos or violins, as well as compose. His instrument, he insisted, was not just a piano or violin, but the entire orchestra. As for using a piano as a tool for composition, he said: "I compose freely and in silence—and I am happy with that. I am not ruled by the tyranny of the fingers, composing only what I can conceive and play on a piano." Berlioz rejoiced that he could compose whatever his imagination suggested, and did not care if "some piano player" complained that his work was too difficult.

Berlioz

He was born on December 11, 1803 in the French village of Saint-Andre in southern France. One of the reasons why he never studied the piano was that his parents, like Schumann's, did not want their son to go into music. "You'll be a doctor," Berlioz' father told him, and refused to encourage him in any other direction. His mother, who was extremely religious, agreed with the father. To her, music was the invention of the devil.

Berlioz hated his studies in medicine. He wrote about his school years in his autobiography: "All that dissection, the dead bodies everywhere, having to stick your hands inside the bowels of another human being. . .what in blazes is so great about that?"

While studying for his degree as a doctor, he tried his hand at musical composition, which was what he really wanted to do. In 1823, a Mass he had composed for one of the churches was performed. It was not successful. He continued his studies in medicine, took his degree in 1824, but then refused to do anything with it.

He had done what his father wanted; he had become a doctor. Now he intended to do what he wanted. After many arguments, he finally persuaded his father to continue to support him while Berlioz studied composition. His father agreed to a one-year trial period. "And that's all," said the father.

In 1825, Berlioz again tried to get his Mass accepted by the public. He borrowed some money to pay for a performance, but the receipts did not equal the production costs, and he went into debt. His father paid Berlioz' debts, but that was the last time. As far as Mr. Berlioz was concerned, his son was more than capable of earning a living, as a doctor.

Wild in Paris

Berlioz was the most mercurial and unpredictable person imaginable. Once in the middle of a concert, he suddenly stood up and yelled from the balcony: "The G *flat,* you idiots, the G *flat,* not the natural! Oh, you brutes, to destroy a work of art with such clumsy playing!" He wasn't too welcome in the theaters of Paris after a few more outbursts like that.

He was temperamental, subject to extreme changes of mood, ecstatic one minute and steeped in melancholy the next. He wasn't copying Schumann, they hadn't met. He was copying Werther, the character in Goethe's story; and he was emulating Byron. Like Schumann, Liszt, Wagner, and many others, Berlioz lived his life as if he were the central figure in one of Goethe's novels or Byron's poems. There was some self-consciousness (there had to be), and possibly even phoniness, in such a romantic posture. These passionate outbursts, moody periods of introspection, and constant gestures were all melodramatic. Mendelssohn, one of the few conservatives in that age, found Berlioz rather trying. "Such uncontrolled enthusiasm is quite unnecessary," he wrote a friend.

When Berlioz was twenty-four years old, he fell in love. In keeping with his Byronic nature, it was a unique and extremely agitated experience. He fell in love with an English actress touring France in a Shakespearean company. Berlioz couldn't speak a word of her language, but he bombarded her with love notes anyway; made many uninvited attempts to visit her; and even sent her gifts. Instead of winning her favor, he only succeeded in scaring the wits out of her. Who was this crazy Frenchman running around declaring his undying love, sending incoherent love notes, and even renting a room next to hers and trying to catch her in the hall? Miss Harriet Smithson made a hasty return to London.

Berlioz carried on quite melodramatically about Harriet even after she left, weeping for her on one friend's shoulder, then raging about her wildly on another's. Once, he even disappeared in the woods outside Paris and made Franz Liszt so worried that Liszt, Chopin, and Mendelssohn went out in search of him. They were afraid he might kill himself, as Werther did in Goethe's romance.

His broken heart proved his best inspiration. One of the two works for which Berlioz is best known was composed within a year after Harriet left France. It was written for her, and about her. Berlioz called his composition the *Fantastic Symphony,* and it was first introduced to Paris on December 5, 1830, a rather important date. Important to Berlioz: Harriet Smithson was once again in Paris.

Symphonie Fantastique

Berlioz wrote out a program for this symphony so that the listeners could understand exactly what he was attempting to say with his music. Though he did not originate program music, it was his *Fantastic Symphony* that brought program music to the fore and gave it a style of its own, emphasizing the contrast with absolute music (music that did not tell a story).

Actually, music cannot tell a story. You can listen to the program music of Berlioz and Liszt, and unless you already know the story behind it, you could never accurately guess what the composer is trying to say. You could detect a waltz here, or a melancholy song there, and probably get the right mood, but the scene you would conjure up in your mind to accompany that mood would most likely be quite different from the actual program.

That does not mean that if you already know the program, hearing the music would be a waste of time. Not at all. Anything that adds to your understanding of the arts can only add to the enjoyment. Such additions to music were very much enjoyed in Berlioz' time.

The story of the *Fantastic Symphony* is about a rejected young lover who turns to opium for relief. But even in an opium stupor, he cannot get the woman he loves (Harriet) out of his mind.

Berlioz put Harriet in the symphony by composing a special melody to represent her. The appearance and reappearance of this melody (the image of Harriet flitting in and out of the young man's mind) is known as the *idée fixe* (fixed idea). This technique of melody manipulation would later be developed into the *leitmotif* by Richard Wagner.

The first movement of the *Fantastic Symphony* is titled "Dreams and Passions" (the young lover is deep in an opium induced sleep), and the music captures the melancholy and joy that love alternately brings. The second movement, called "The Ball," is a vibrant waltz; the melody of Harriet is played hauntingly by the woodwinds. The third movement shows the influence of Beethoven's semiprogrammatic "Pastoral" Symphony; here the English horn and oboe introduce tranquil music. This movement is called "Scenes in the Country." The fourth movement, "The March to the Gallows," is a vigorous and brilliant march, often excerpted for concert performances. The lover has dreamed that he has killed Harriet and must pay for it with his own life. The fifth movement, "The Witches' Sabbath," is a satanic use of a hymn from the Catholic mass for the dead, the *Dies Irae* (Day of Wrath). Franz Liszt, greatly impressed by this symphony, used the *Dies Irae* similarly in the "Inferno" movement of his *Dante Symphony*.

Berlioz' symphony was unique, not only because it brought program music into fashion, but also because it brought a new type of orchestra into fashion. To get the powerful sound the symphony needed, Berlioz expanded the orchestra to an unprecedented size. In the string section alone there were sixty musicians, four times the normal number. Berlioz seemed to relish the irony of it, a man who couldn't play one instrument changing the whole concept of the symphony orchestra.

Byron Again

The symphony did nothing for Berlioz as far as Harriet Smithson was concerned. The English actress didn't even realize it was being performed, even though he had chosen the date just for her.

But the concert was important in a far greater way. It was a huge success, first of all, justifying Berlioz' decision to become a composer; and its influence was enormous. It inspired Franz Liszt, who was present in the audience that first night, to follow in the direction that Berlioz was taking; and Liszt in turn would influence Wagner. Unfortunately for Berlioz, this would turn out to be another instance in which the pupils ultimately cast their teacher into the shadows.

A subsequent performance of the *Fantastic Symphony* found Niccolo Paganini in the audience. The virtuoso violinist was so impressed that he commissioned Berlioz to compose a work especially for him.

The Paganini composition was called *Harold in Italy*, a symphonic rendering of Byron's autobiographical poem. Berlioz seldom strayed from the literature of Byron, Goethe, or Shakespeare. Paganini was annoyed because Berlioz did not write the concerto as he had expected, so it was several years before he paid Berlioz for his troubles. When Paganini finally consented to hear *Harold in Italy*, he was deeply moved. "You rank with Beethoven," he wrote Berlioz apologetically, including in his generous letter an equally generous bank draft, which freed Berlioz for an entire year from financial worries.

When Achievements Mock

Berlioz had tried for a long time, since studying to be a doctor, to win the Prix de Rome, a three-year scholarship to study music in Rome. Finally, after five attempts, he won it and was sent to Italy. It was to be anticlimactic: he did not like Italy. He was not a traditionalist and decided that he did not want to study the Italian style after all. "That was Mozart's problem," the irrepressible Berlioz declared, "too much Italy."

Berlioz did not complete his three year stay in Italy. He returned in 1832 and, to his delight, found that Harriet Smithson was once more in Paris. Berlioz had not gotten over her, and he could not be persuaded to stop trying to get her attention. He again arranged for his *Fantastic Symphony* to be performed, and he beseeched her to attend. This time perseverance paid off. She went to the concert, listened to his music, and was completely conquered. In October of the following year, Berlioz married the heroine of his symphony.

He created another symphony for Harriet: his *Romeo and Juliet*. This symphonic work is vocal, as well as instrumental. It is a dramatic symphony, somewhat like Mendelssohn's *Elijah* (more an oratorio than a symphony). It tells the well-known story of the feud between the Capulets and Montagues, and how it took the death of the young lovers to unite them. The music that Berlioz composed for the balcony scene when Romeo and Juliet pledge their love, is a beautiful and intense duet; Romeo is represented by the deep and rich violas and cellos, and Juliet by the melodious and stirring woodwinds. Its performance at the Paris Conservatory in 1839 was a great success. Unhappily, the marriage that inspired it was less successful.

The marriage between Berlioz and Harriet did not work out. In fact, it turned out to be an opium nightmare, just like the last movement in the *Fantastic Symphony*. They were both too temperamental, he a tyrant, she a shrew, and they were both having trouble with their careers. Harriet turned to wines and whiskeys and became an alcoholic, to forget that her acting career was over. Berlioz turned to opium to forget Harriet and the disastrous financial situation that his overorchestrated symphonies were creating. He had to pay the salaries of the musicians out of his own pocket, when the door receipts failed to produce enough to cover the production costs.

In 1846, for instance, Berlioz' *Damnation of Faust,* another new form of his devising, was performed to a small, and not very enthusiastic, audience. The *Faust* composition has been called everything from an opera to an oratorio. Actually, it is a vocal work in four parts, each section dealing with an important scene from Geothe's *Faust.* A few of the orchestral pieces are quite popular, and the ballet scenes are performed frequently. Unfortunately, when it was first performed, it cost Berlioz 10,000 francs, about 2,000 dollars. After that, he was never out of debt.

Progressives in Paris

It is not surprising that France produced such innovators as Berlioz. The literary and musical activity that was taking place in France was making Paris the cultural center of the world. That activity was more than matched by the developments taking place in painting. Young painters like Gericault and Delacroix reacted against the cold formalism of the classicists and brought bright color, vitality, and romantic emotion into their creations.

The philosophy of individualism spread rapidly, and there were soon several groups of artists with opposing theories about painting. One group turned to legend and mythology for their subjects; another painted historical events and characters; yet another turned to nature and concentrated on landscapes and farm workers. The history of art in this period becomes a history of individuals and their many experimental and complementary styles. Jean Baptiste Corot painted misty and poetic nature scenes; Jean Francois Millet used his canvas to turn the humble peasants of the French farmlands into symbols of strength and independence; Gustave Courbet painted the same peasants but kept his canvas free of sentimentality. "My paintings will show people what is wrong with the world," Courbet said.

In the last third of the nineteenth century, the impressionist movement began, led by Claude Monet, Edgar Degas, and Camille Pissarro. Using "broken" color, instead of solid brush strokes, these painters brought a variety and brilliance to their art that was wholly unique. They wanted to capture those fleeting moments that flash impressionistically across one's vision, and their technique of juxtaposing various dashes of color achieved this aim perfectly. This style would eventually influence such notables as Gauguin, Van Gogh, Renoir, and Cezanne. Paintings like Van Gogh's "Starry Night" and Cezanne's "Mont Saint-Victoire," with their brilliant colors and unique use of line and structure, opened the way for even more changes. Cubism and abstraction would become the next wave in this ever expanding and constantly changing art. Paris was certainly a place for progressive individuals.

Techniques and Contributions

Berlioz was the first consistently romantic symphony composer. He brought autobiography into composition through the musical expression of incidents in his own life and imagination. To capture all the complexities of his life, he expanded the orchestra, adding more and different instruments to capture the tone and color he wanted.

Before Berlioz began to experiment with the orchestra, the standard size of this musical group was about thirty to fifty players. On occasion Berlioz demanded more than 100 players for his compositions. His ideal orchestra was close to 500 players! "If an orchestra is well-balanced, well-rehearsed, and well-led, it can be as big as man's imagination can conceive," he insisted.

He was not a melodist like Chopin and Schumann, but his introduction of the *idee fixe*, the technique that brings a melody back time and again throughout the composition, had great influence.

His strength lies in his orchestration, the harmonics and color effects he was able to achieve. He was always trying out new instrumental combinations, hoping to achieve as many different and exciting color effects as possible. He also helped introduce the English horn into the symphony, and his emphasis on the harp helped make it one of the permanent instruments in the orchestra.

Along with the other early romantic composers, Berlioz was an innovator in rhythm, using a number of contrasting rhythms in his work, to create sudden and unexpected shifts in mood.

Leader of the Band

Berlioz' sense of drama carried over to the conductor's podium, where he began almost a new art: the virtuoso conductor. He was very fussy about the performance of his works. He was even known to violently attack musicians who dared to play his compositions poorly. "I will conduct my own works," he declared. "And woe to anyone who does not play it perfectly." In 1842, Berlioz began tours all over Europe and Russia, conducting his own works in all the capital cities for as long as his money held out. He was as dynamic a conductor as he was a composer, and he was quite popular in some cities, more popular to watch than to listen to.

There are two opposing views of the symphony conductor: 1) he represents a unifying force, without which the orchestra couldn't operate; 2) he is an egotistical showoff who takes most of the credit, and the orchestra could perform just as well without his presence.

There is a lot to be said for both views. It is true that modern orchestras, numbering over 100 musicians operate more effectively if there is only one leader among them. Someone must decide what tempo should be employed, or how much fortissimo a certain dynamic passage should receive, and whether or not everybody is playing at the right time.

Once all that is decided must there be someone standing in front of the orchestra while they are playing, gyrating and waving his arms for one or two hours? Can't he sit down once he's gotten things started? Many people think so, especially when the orchestra is playing music that they have performed over and over again through the years.

But since Berlioz, the ultradramatic conductor has become almost an institution. The man who couldn't play a musical instrument himself found a way to take the credit for everyone else's virtuosity.

A Light Eclipsed

As Paganini noted, Berlioz was the first composer to take up where Beethoven left off, to continue the break with classical forms. More than anyone before him, Berlioz linked literature to the musical arts, establishing the program symphony as an alternative to the absolute music of the previous period. As the man who influenced Liszt and Wagner, Berlioz was most responsible for "The Music of the Future," the avant-garde school of musicians who were so determined to break completely with the music of the past.

Yet Berlioz' compositions were not generally accepted. Paying to get them performed ruined him financially. He had to turn to fields other than composing to support himself. In 1853, he accepted the position as music critic for a Paris journal. For ten years he earned most of his income from writing rather than from composing.

In 1862, Berlioz finally had that one last success he was looking for. His opera, *Beatrice and Benedict* (based on Shakespeare's *Much Ado About Nothing*), was a great hit. It was an extraordinary achievement. His finances were in utter collapse; a second marriage had turned out worse than his marriage to Harriet; his early works, which had won him some acclaim, were totally eclipsed by the music of Liszt and Wagner. Despite all this, he managed to compose a comic opera.

It was only a brief return to what had been only a brief glory. Berlioz was ill physically. He withdrew from society and lived in self-isolation in a small Paris apartment, still fancying himself a character in one of Byron's poems.

He turned to opium in his last years to relieve the sense of defeat he felt. There was no chance for him after that. On March 8, 1869, his Byronic spirit was finally at peace.

Study Activities

1. Suppose you wanted to compose some program music for the Battle of Lexington. What rhythms, tempo, dynamics, and instrumentation would you use?

    Rhythm/Tempo (march, dance, fast, slow, moderate, etc.)
    Dynamics (loud, soft, crescendo, etc.)
    Expression/Mood (anger, martial, sweet, joyous, etc.)
    Instruments (full orchestra, strings, woodwinds, combination of. . .)

THE BATTLE OF LEXINGTON

Event	Rhythm/Tempo	Dynamics	Mood	Instrumentation
Sam Adams gives speech at Lexington.				
British send large force to capture him.				
Paul Revere makes his famous ride from Charlestown to Lexington to warn the Americans.				
Eight hundred British soldiers confront seventy Americans at Lexington.				
Eight Americans are dead on the battlefield.				
The British go to Concord. Four hundred Americans drive them back to Boston.				
American farmers leave their farms to fight British as they retreat.				
The Americans celebrate their victory with songs and prayer.				

2. Do some library research on one of the following French composers and make a class report or write a brief paper about his life and music.

   Edouard Lalo (1823-1892)
   Camille Saint-Saëns (1835-1921)

3. Is it fair that the conductor gets so much credit? Is it the conductor that makes the orchestra famous, or the orchestra that makes the conductor famous? How can the 100 individual musicians who actually make the musical sounds get to share equally in the credit? Or should they?

4. Choose one of the impressionists (Manet, Pissarro, Sisley, Monet, Degas, Renoir, etc.), and write a report on his life and work. Try to bring in some posters of his work or an art book with some of his pictures in it.

5. There were two famous women impressionists, Berthe Morisot and Mary Cassatt. Because women artists have not received the same critical attention as men, you might want to do special studies of Morisot's and Cassatt's lives and works.

VI

Franz Liszt:
The Spirit and the Flesh

Liszt

Franz Liszt was born in Hungary in 1811. Like Chopin and Mendelssohn, he was a child prodigy, performing marvels at the piano that made him famous at a very early age.

His father, a steward in the service of the Esterhazys, was very much like Mozart's father. He recognized his son's talent early, and did all he could to develop that talent and bring it to the attention of those who could further it. He knew that, with the right patronage, his son could surpass anyone then performing in the musical world.

When he was nine years old, young Liszt played for the Esterhazy family. They and their wealthy friends were so impressed that a special fund was set up to pay for his education in Vienna.

In Vienna, Liszt studied with the great piano teacher Karl Czerny, whose piano exercises are still considered among the most important today. The boy's playing was so good that the teacher refused to accept any money. "It is pleasure enough for me just to teach him," Czerny said. Before Liszt left Vienna, he met the great Beethoven. Beethoven attended a concert where Liszt was playing. When he heard the marvelous things the boy could do with a piano, he went up to him and kissed him. It was the ultimate tribute any beginning musician could receive.

He went to Paris in 1823, hoping to study at the Conservatory. Enrollment was limited then to native Frenchmen, so Liszt had to go to private teachers. He could not get into the French Conservatory, but he could get into the hearts of the French people. Everyone who heard him perform was amazed by his virtuosity. When he traveled to London that same year, earning large sums of money at each recital, he just as easily won the hearts and admiration of the British.

Though their careers were parallel, and they met each other several times, Liszt was not like Mendelssoh in temperament, he was not able to handle the fame and adoration that came his way with the same ease and

and coolness; some called him a gypsy. He wanted to experience as much as he could, to indulge all his senses and truly feel life at its fullest. He was romantic in outlook and in action. His zest for life was infectious, and most people who came into contact with him went away feeling happier and more alive.

His unorthodox life style caused his parents a great deal of concern: especially his relationship with the ladies. Liszt was very handsome and charming; both young girls and older women were attracted to him, and he to them. From the age of fifteen, he was constantly getting involved in wild love affairs, causing no end of gossip among the gossip-loving Parisians.

It was a cheerful and exciting life the young boy led. By the talent in his own hands, he had risen from the obscure position of a servant's son to become one of the most sought-after child performers in Europe. It seemed that there was nothing to worry about in life, that he could reach out and take all he wanted from it.

It is no surprise, then, that the sudden death of Franz' father in 1827, when Franz was only sixteen, came as a tremendous shock to him. The death of such a close and dearly-loved person made life seem a lot less frivolous.

When he recovered from his deep sorrow, he did some serious thinking. Liszt decided to renounce his present life. He contemplated taking religious orders, but his family talked him out of it. He did give up music though, and he gave up women. He spent the next four years reading and studying books on religion, literature, and history.

Encounter with Paganini

When he was twenty, Liszt came into contact with three people who would make him reconsider his renunciation of music. He met Frederic Chopin, who had just moved to Paris from Poland and was creating a sensation with his own unique piano style in the aristocratic *salons* that Liszt frequented; he attended the first performance of Hector Berlioz' *Fantastic Symphony* and was extremely impressed by Berlioz' dynamic, and even thunderous, orchestration. Liszt suddenly felt that he could bring forth from the piano new sonorities and sounds, if he were to approach that instrument with the same intensity Berlioz approached his orchestra. It was the first time in years he had felt so moved, and his vows to stay away from music were weakened. Then Liszt met Paganini. He went to see the violinist perform and was held spellbound by the Italian's amazing virtuosity.

Nicolo Paganini (1782-1840) was the greatest violinist of all times. He could make his listeners believe he was playing two violins at once, plucking the strings with his left hand and bowing with his right. He was so adept at getting music out of his instrument that some people insisted he had sold his soul to the devil.

Paganini was not just a virtuoso; he was also a composer. In order to display what he could do with his fingers and the bow, he created some of the most difficult and complex violin music ever conceived, music filled with double-stops and brilliant harmonics. He was only sixteen years old when he composed his series of *Caprices.* Only *he* had enough dexterity to play them properly. Because he feared competition, he did not allow all his works to be published during his lifetime. When they were made public, only the most accomplished violinist could do anything with them.

Paganini was the superstar of the nineteenth century. Wherever he went, he was mobbed by admirers; and he went everywhere. By the time he died in 1840, he had amassed a fortune from his concerts totaling a half-million dollars.

When Franz Liszt heard him play, and then heard the thunderous roar of the approving audience, all his previous ambitions to be a great musician were renewed.

The New Liszt

Liszt had no intention of taking up where he had left off. He had decided to recreate his whole image. He took popular symphonic works and made transcriptions of them for the piano, writing in such dazzling cadenzas and harmonics that the piano sounded as if it were duplicating the entire orchestra. He added a flourish to his every playing gesture, and brought the dramatic arts to the concert hall.

His return to the concert stage in 1833 was everything he had dreamed; he absolutely conquered the public. When he went on stage, he addressed himself completely to the audience. Like an actor, he would toss his head back, his long hair flowing gracefully, and his eyes would search out the audience as if he meant to mesmerize them.

And mesmerize them he did. No instrument, not even the violin, can match the spectrum of sound that the piano can produce; and Franz Liszt was the first person to fully use the piano's potential. Before his "rebirth," performers usually worked in groups, as in vaudeville, where one act followed another. It was Liszt who originated the piano recital as we know it today, a performance given by a single person. He did not feel that he had to share the stage with any other artist, and he was right. He soon had the stage entirely to himself, and he never failed to give his audiences an incomparable theatrical treat. He became a legend at the age of twenty-five, and managed to sustain that legend throughout the next fifty years, another incomparable theatrical feat.

He imitated Paganini in other things, too. When he went back to music, he also went back to women. Liszt became involved with the Countess D'Agoult, and their affair caused a sensation, particularly when the Countess deserted her husband and three children and ran off to Switzerland with the ardent pianist. Liszt and the Countess had three children of their own before the affair was ended. One of their children, Cosima, would someday create a similar sensation by deserting her husband to run off with the composer Richard Wagner.

Piano Compositions

Liszt gained a great deal from his association with Chopin; here was the other extreme of the romantic temperament. Berlioz was fire and storm, Paganini was style and flair, and Chopin was soul-stirring sensitivity. To combine these elements, the fire of Berlioz, the flair of Paganini, and the finesse of Chopin, was Liszt's challenge.

Liszt transcribed Paganini's *Caprices* for the piano, writing in more than just the complex and finger-twisting effects that only he could play. He succeeded in capturing the spirit of Paganini in these pieces, while stamping the work with his own musical signature. The cadenzas, harmonies, and skill in melody manipulation are unmistakably Liszt's.

Also from Paganini came the inspiration for "La Campanella," where "little bells" are heard in a charming demonstration of contrasts, the right hand high on the upper octaves, while the left is sounding out the bass.

Of his piano music, Liszt is best known for his Hungarian Rhapsodies (he was the first to create the rhapsodic form), which are extremely popular and constantly played at recitals. They are fast-paced, lyrical, and hard to resist. For the most part, these rhapsodies are based on gypsy melodies and rhythms; they offer sharp contrasts. Sometimes a skipping melody might suddenly be replaced by a warm, yearning gypsy love song, made especially poignant by the Hungarian minor scale (A, B, C, D-sharp, E, F, G-sharp, A).

One of the most popular piano pieces in the world, "Liebestraum," meaning "Dream of Love," was written by Liszt. It is a simple, beautiful song-like melody, repeated numerous times in different octaves against a sparkling background of cadenzas.

Surprisingly, Liszt only composed two piano concertos (Mozart by comparison composed dozens of them). Chopin also only wrote two concertos, but he was not drawn toward large forms as Liszt was.

It is more surprising to find that only one of Liszt's two concertos is very good; and that one, the *Concerto No. 1,* was poorly received for many years, even with Liszt at the keyboard. It is hard to understand why. It is very dynamic, with good representation of all the instruments, not just the piano. The flutes, clarinets, and strings have especially noteworthy parts. The piano is superb throughout, its melodies forceful and commanding at times, sweet and lyrical at others. It took almost twenty years before this concerto became established in the recital repertory, but since then, it has been a favored showpiece.

From Russia With Love

Liszt was forever getting involved with women. His affair with the Countess D'Agoult, which lasted from 1833 until 1840, had shocked Europe. Then in 1847, on a concert tour of Russia, Liszt met the highly eccentric Princess Carolyne Wittgenstein. Again, he was in love with a married woman. When she asked her husband for a divorce (which he would never give her), it almost caused an international incident, the son of a Hungarian servant breaking up a prince's marriage.

It is a wonder what Liszt saw in her, other than the small fact that she was fabulously wealthy and one step above the Countess in the social register! The Princess was a neurotic. She had an irrational fear of fresh air, a rather unusual phobia. She stayed indoors as much as possible in fetid, airtight rooms. In those rooms, she would smoke strong black cigars, one after another, until the room was cloud of comforting black smoke. She was homely and manly, demanding and possessive, and a religious fanatic. She constantly talked about, and worked on, her "life's project," a twenty-four-volume discussion of the most tedious aspects of religious dogma imaginable. But despite all of this, the Princess was the best thing that could have happened to Liszt.

For ten years, Liszt traveled across Europe and Russia giving concerts. He was in demand more than any other composer-performer and virtually ruled the concert halls.

But in 1847, when he was thirty-six years old, Liszt decided to spend more time on his compositions. The Princess had convinced him that he had a lot more to offer posterity than piano works. He retired from his career as a concert pianist and accepted a lucrative post at Weimar as Kapellmeister.

The Tone Poems

The Princess followed Liszt to Weimar. Her influence on him for the next decade brought him closer and closer to the church, but also closer to becoming one of the great composers in history. During his ten-year stay at Weimar (1848-1858), she encouraged him to compose most of his orchestral works.

Liszt was influenced by Berlioz' program music and wanted to follow in that direction. He liked to improve upon anything he imitated, so he developed a new concept in program music, which he called the symphonic poem, or tone poem.

The main difference between the tone poem as Liszt conceived it, and the program symphony which inspired it, is that the tone poem is usually complete in one movement. Liszt saw an opportunity to break away more completely from the classical school, which had established multimovement symphonies as the predominant form. It was a timely innovation; the tone poem quickly became one of the most popular forms of orchestral composition, and remained so through the first quarter of the twentieth century.

Liszt's symphonic poems (he composed twelve of them) were inspired by anything: a play, a poem, an idea. His most famous is *Les Preludes,* which ranks among the most popular orchestral works ever written. It is a heroic work, with a flowing melody that builds up a tremendous musical tension. Liszt's use of crescendo and decrescendo in this poem is the ultimate in dynamics. You can see in the following excerpt how the music sweeps upward in a soaring melody:

The poem depicts the striking contrasts of quiet and storm that exist in every man's life. Liszt presents a storm in the music, but it is not a storm that frightens; rather it is one that challenges, that makes a person want to match his or her strength against the forces of nature. "Man can regain in combat the complete consciousness of himself and the complete command of his powers," Liszt wrote in the program.

PROGRAM FOR *LES PRELUDES*

Life is but a series of preludes to an unknown song,
a song where death strikes the first note. Love is an
enchanted dawn, but there is no love that is not interrupted by some storm.

Man turns to nature to renew his spirit when the storms
have cruelly wounded him. But he cannot hide in nature.
When the trumpet sounds the call to battle, when life
again beckons with all its perils, man must courageously
ready himself to once more meet the challenge. Man can
regain in combat the complete consciousness of himself
and the complete command of his powers.

The other tone poems of Liszt that are played today are *Tasso* and *Mazeppa,* the first based on one of Goethe's plays, *Mazeppa* taken from Victor Hugo's poem.

Two Souls, Alas!

Liszt's two symphonies were composed in Weimar. Their subject matter reflects the religious direction his mind was taking.

The *Dante Symphony,* in two movements, represents Liszt's version of the "Inferno" and "Purgatorio." The harshness and desolation that the music depicts are relieved by a vocal section at the end of the symphony (linking it with Beethoven's *Ninth,* which set the precedent for choral works in the last movement). Liszt, torn between his desire to go on at Weimar, and the constant pressuring by Princess Wittgenstein for him to take holy orders, ended the *Dante Symphony* with a religious choral section, a Magnificat.

His *Faust Symphony* is by far the more interesting of the two. The first movement represents Faust. There are two main themes to portray the two sides of his nature. "Two souls, alas!, reside within my breast," says Faust in Goethe's poem. "One reaches to the heavens, the other to the dust." The music is stormy and clearly shows Faust's troubled personality. Those who knew Liszt well, believed that the first movement was autobiographical. Certainly, Liszt was torn between two worlds.

The second movement uses the woodwinds and viola to portray Gretchen. It is a melancholy movement, reminding the listener of Gretchen's sad fate.

The third movement, "Mephistopheles," is another innovation of Liszt's. Instead of searching for a theme to fit the devil, he uses the two Faust themes in distorted shapes to show that the devil is a part of man himself, and also to show that the devil cannot create (he cannot have themes of his own), he can only negate. Faust's themes, negated as they are in broken fragments, represent Mephistopheles.

At the end of Goethe's play, Faust's soul is saved by the intervention of Gretchen. Woman's love becomes symbolic of God's love. Liszt uses a male chorus at the end of his symphony to sing the closing lines of Goethe's play: "The Eternal Feminine draws us ever onward."

A Rival for Center Stage

Liszt was the archromantic in music, and Percy Bysshe Shelley (1792-1822) was the archromantic in word-music, poetry, surpassing even Byron in his often wild and adventurous ways.

Shelley was an aristocrat by birth. Like his friend Lord Byron, Shelley was more interested in the common man and his problems than in maintaining personal titles. He was one of the most radical thinkers of his day, proposing an atheistic and even communistic society fifty years before anyone ever heard of Karl Marx.

Like Liszt, Shelley was concerned with the larger questions of life: beauty, fate, and universal love. Shelley believed in the ultimate perfectability of man, and his poems, like Liszt's music, are at times prophetic. His long verse drama, *Prometheus Unbound,* shows what man can be when he uses love instead of tyranny.

Shelley was essentially a lyrical poet, using language that was most melodious. One of his greatest strengths was his ability to create concrete pictures of abstract or insubstantial things such as beauty, fate, and death. This was also Liszt's challenge: to take abstract music and make it "speak" as clearly and concretely as possible.

A good friend of John Keats, Shelley was deeply moved by his death and wrote the long and beautiful elegy *Adonis.* He took the story from the Greek legend, where the youth Adonis, beloved by Aphrodite, the goddess of love, was killed by a wild boar. To Shelley, the critics who viciously attacked Keats' poetry, and the unappreciative public, were the wild boars. But like Adonis, who was brought back to life by one of the other Greek goddesses, Keats will live on forever, too. Here is a part of that elegy; you can see how easily Liszt might have turned it into a tone poem:

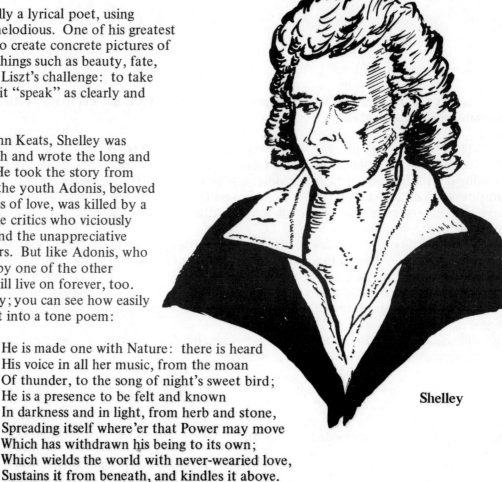

Shelley

He is made one with Nature: there is heard
His voice in all her music, from the moan
Of thunder, to the song of night's sweet bird;
He is a presence to be felt and known
In darkness and in light, from herb and stone,
Spreading itself where'er that Power may move
Which has withdrawn his being to its own;
Which wields the world with never-wearied love,
Sustains it from beneath, and kindles it above.

The Sublimation of the Ego

For the ten years that he was at Weimar, Liszt put aside his own ego and dedicated himself to helping other musicians. His orchestra conducted many premieres, and a number of young, aspiring composers went to Weimar to get their works performed.

Liszt also insisted that the works of Berlioz, Schumann, and Wagner, which were being ignored in other cities, be performed in Weimar. What Mendelssohn did for Leipzig earlier in the century, Liszt did for Weimar, making it one of the cultural centers of Europe.

Producing the works of Richard Wagner was Liszt's favorite project. For some time, the composer Wagner had been in disrepute, not only musically, but politically. He had taken an active part in the Revolution of 1848, and when the revolution failed, he was forced to flee to Switzerland. He went first to Franz Liszt who, without any hesitation, agreed to hide him from the German authorities. Their many talks about music, literature, and politics convinced Liszt of the importance of Wagner's vision. For the next ten years, he promoted Wagner's new German operas. When the Duke of Weimar refused to give Liszt funds to produce any more of Wagner's operas, which were rather expensive, Liszt resigned his post.

For some time Liszt had been thinking of changing his life-style completely, so the argument with the Duke over Wagner was really a pretense for Liszt to leave. As he had once been, after his father's death, Liszt was again drawn to the religious life. In 1865, he traveled to Rome and went to the Order of St. Francis of Assisi. He told the church authorities that he would devote the rest of his life to helping others, especially young musicians. He was accepted in the Order, and from then on he wore the cassock of an abbé.

Abbe Liszt was not one to remove himself totally from the world. He divided his time between living in Rome and in Weimar, with occasional visits to the capitals of Europe. While he studied religion, he continued to teach the piano to any gifted person who approached him. He never charged a fee. He also kept working on his compositions, most of which were now religious in tone, for the next twenty years of life that remained to him.

He was happy during those years. His spiritual longings were now satisfied, although not at the expense of the physical (he kept getting into trouble with women until he died at the age of seventy-five). He had made a significant contribution to the development of music. He had been influenced by many, but he had in turn become a greater influence. "Since becoming acquainted with Franz Liszt's music," wrote Wagner in 1859, "my own treatment of harmony has greatly changed." He had lived a full, and at times glorious, life. He was content when his time finally came to leave the stage.

The Romantic Matrix

Liszt was acquainted with all the early romantics, Chopin, Mendelssohn, Schumann, and Berlioz. Let us compare these composers within the framework of a romantic matrix. It should be interesting to see who best fits into the mold.

INDIVIDUALISM

Chopin rebukes the Czar of Russia.
Mendelssohn single-handedly revives Bach and the baroque era.
Schumann starts his own music journal.
Berlioz doubles the size of the orchestra.
Liszt consciously turns himself into the greatest superstar in Europe.

CREATING NEW FORMS

Chopin expands the piano repertory.
Mendelssohn prefers classical forms.
Schumann composes character pieces.
Berlioz creates the program symphony.
Liszt creates symphonic poems, rhapsodies, and virtuoso recitals.

EMOTIONALISM/SUBJECTIVITY

Chopin's nocturnes and impromptus evoke immediate responses.
Mendelssohn's *Hebrides Overture* is filled with sensuous dynamics.
Schumann's intense emotionalism drives him insane.
Berlioz gives up a scholarship after trying for five years to get it.
Liszt's intense piano playing causes women in his audiences to swoon.

LOVE OF NATURE

Chopin prefers the Paris salons to the countryside.
Mendelssohn's symphonies capture the many moods of the Italian landscape.
Schumann captures the freshness of life in his *Spring Symphony.*
Berlioz prefers literature as his source of inspiration.
Liszt depicts both storms and pastoral scenes in his tone poems.

NATIONALISM

Chopin brings Polish rhythms and melodies into this work.
Mendelssohn begins Leipzig Conservatory.
Schumann sets German poems to music.
Berlioz is more international than national.
Liszt makes Hungarian rhapsodies popular.

It appears that Franz Liszt and Robert Schumann are the only two who fulfill all of the above categories without exception. But all of the above is a matter of *quantity*. When it comes to deciding who the greatest romantic is on a *qualitative* basis, no one person can really say. Certainly, no matrix will ever decide the issue.

Study Activities

1. The section titled "Piano Compositions" in this chapter refers to the Hungarian minor scale. Draw a musical staff and write out the scale, properly indicating the sharps.

2. Imagine you have the following instruments at your disposal for the composition of a romantic symphony, one in which you want to express the conflicting moods of love, sorrow, and anger.

STRINGS	WOODWINDS	BRASS	PERCUSSION
Violins	Flutes	French horn	Drums
Violas	Oboe	English horn	Cymbals
Cellos	Clarinets	Trumpets	Gong
Double Bass	Bassoon	Trombones	Triangle
Harp	Contrabassoon	Tuba	

Without composing music itself, lay out a "paper" symphony. Which instrument will introduce your main theme? What combinations will represent the "love" *leitmotif*, etc?

3. Define the word "music" in terms of a Mozart symphony; redefine the word in terms of a Liszt tone poem; then define "music" one final time to cover the atonal works of Arnold Schoenberg.

4. What American legend or historical event would you set to music? How many movements would you have? How would they be titled? Would you use *leitmotifs?*

VII

Richard Wagner:

The Master Singer

Wagner was born in Leipzig, Germany in 1813. Like Berlioz, he was never a musical performer. He had some piano lessons when he was twelve, but didn't keep them up. As an example of his ambitious nature, though, he had only learned a few basic finger exercises when he sat down and tried to play an entire opera score.

Wagner's first interest was in literature. He wrote poems and plays when he was young, and he thought he would become a writer. But when he was fifteen years old, he attended a performance of Beethoven's *Ninth Symphony* and of his opera *Fidelio,* and Wagner knew from that moment that he, too, would be a great composer.

Instead of doing the usual thing and getting the proper instruction from teachers, Wagner learned music mostly on his own. He spent his time studying the scores of all of Beethoven's symphonies and over-tures, analyzing them and making transcripts for the piano. His first musical friend was Friedrich Wieck, the tyrannical father of Clara. Wieck supplied the budding composer with scores and occasionally corrected Wagner's initial attempts at composing.

Wagner attended the University of Leipzig. He exhibited a love more for gambling and drinking than for studying. Except for his philosophy and music studies, he all but ignored his academic curriculum. He had a taste for expensive clothes, insisted on dining at the best restaurants, and spent large sums on his girlfriends. When his money ran out (which was often), he would borrow from his friends or try to win some through gambling. He was frequently borrowing and seldom paying back. He carried these extravagances through life, constantly living beyond his means and expecting others to pay his bills. He had, as he said, "a great destiny," and couldn't be worried about such trifles as money. Long before he had achieved any worldly success, when he was still a young man, Wagner was positive he would be famous.

Wagner

Theodore Weinlig, the cantor of St. Thomas, instructed Wagner in music theory. In six months, Wagner had absorbed all that Weinlig could show him. Under Weinlig's direction, he composed several orchestral works, a few of which were performed by the local orchestra. And one, Weinlig managed to get published. It was a small success, but enough to fuel his ambitions and justify his self-confidence.

Minna, Money, and Megalomania

In 1833, Wagner managed to get the small post of choirmaster at the Würzburger Theater. He only lasted a year. His gambling and high living put him seriously into debt. In order to escape his creditors, he fled to Magdeburg, where he became the conductor of the local opera.

Wagner was now composing operas. He found, to his dismay, though, that the public did not particularly care for his work, at least not in Magdeburg. In 1836, a performance of his opera, *Forbidden Love,* was such a financial failure that it actually brought about the bankruptcy of the opera house and the loss of his job.

While in Magdeburg, he fell in love with an actress named Minna Planer. When she went to Königsberg, he followed her, and they were married. Minna had an acting job, and they lived off her salary. They went deeply into debt.

Wagner did not have a very happy life with Minna. Almost from the day he married her, he regretted it. She did not share his ambitions, could not understand his music, and failed to give him the constant encouragement that his inflated ego craved. As a result, Wagner was forever seeking affection from other women. He often got involved with the daughters or wives of his friends, which, in turn, resulted in the loss of his friends.

In 1837, Wagner and Minna were living in Russia, in the city of Riga. He was the conductor of the Riga Opera House. The Wagners continued to spend more than they earned. If they saw an item of furniture they liked, they bought it; if Minna wanted a new dress or some jewelry, she bought it; if Wagner had a sudden yen for champagne and caviar, he bought it by the case. Everything they bought put them deeper into debt. Their credit became so bad that the shopkeepers rebelled against them, protested to the authorities, and had Wagner dismissed from his post.

Their bad habits caught up with them in Paris, where they took refuge after their troubles in Russia. They quickly exhausted their credit in Paris (the French shopkeepers were too shrewd for them) and found themselves in an incredibly difficult situation. From 1839 until 1843, the Wagners lived from hand to mouth, taking in boarders, hiding from their numerous creditors, and fighting off the spectre of starvation. More than once, Wagner was actually put into prison for not paying his bills. He felt harassed, demeaned, and couldn't understand that he had brought it upon himself, or wouldn't admit it. He blamed the shopkeepers, the landlords, his "miserly" friends, and ranted about a capitalist system and the "Jewish money-grubbers who were all conspiring against him." He became an intense anti-Semite, and his writings about the Jews would have fearful results in the twentieth century.

Wagner blamed everybody for his troubles but himself. He was suffering from megalomania, he had delusions of grandeur. His creditors, and anyone who didn't agree with him, were no more than "puny gnats" biting at his noble skin, and one day he would stand high above them all.

In the meantime, Minna polished the boarders' shoes and Wagner took hack jobs, transcribing and arranging music scores for solo instruments and writing a newspaper article on occasion. He was still a long way from achieving the grandeur he envisioned for himself.

Persistence Often Pays

Wagner kept on composing, just as sure of himself as ever. In 1840, he had a brief moment of hope when the director of the Paris Opera purchased his libretto for *The Flying Dutchman,* but that turned out to be humiliating also. The director only wanted the story from Wagner; another composer was commissioned to write the music.

Wagner had little choice but to sell his libretto. He desperately needed the 500 francs that the story brought. He was still determined to write his own music for it, and he did, though it wouldn't be performed for some years yet to come.

When Wagner first arrived in Paris, he went to see Meyerbeer, whose spectacle-operas were being performed everywhere. Wagner wanted Meyerbeer to see an opera he had composed called *Rienzi.* It was a large opera in five acts, much in the style of the French grand opera and Meyerbeer's own. The older composer good-naturedly looked over Wagner's opera. He liked it and introduced Wagner to several influential people. No one accepted the opera for production, and Wagner was unable to make use of his new acquaintances other than to borrow money from them.

Finally, after so many years of disappointments, the Dresden Opera, on Meyerbeer's recommendation, accepted *Rienzi.* In order to get to Dresden to see his own opera, Wagner had to borrow the necessary funds to pay for his and Minna's trip.

Rienzi was an instant and huge success. Suddenly, Wagner had the fame he had for so long anticipated. It was sweet at first to savor the success, he had so few up until then. Now everyone was calling him Maestro and asking about his next work. Wagner bitterly remembered the misery of those four years in Paris, and how he had single-handedly carved out this victory (he so easily forgot Meyerbeer), and he grew hard and ungrateful. This success would encourage him to write some of the world's greatest music; but as far as his personality was concerned, it only made things worse.

One After Another

The Dresden Opera next performed *The Flying Dutchman,* which was also successful with the audience. The story is based on a legend about a man condemned to sail the seas forever, until he is redeemed by the love of a woman. Wagner began to establish his own style with this opera, dealing with a subject related to the German identity, and creating music that dramatically underscored the plot. *The Flying Dutchman* only lasted for a few performances, but enough to rate it a success.

In 1843, Wagner was asked to take over as musical director of the Dresden Opera. When his creditors in Leipzig, Magdeburg, Königsberg, Riga and Paris found out he had a permanent job, they flocked to Dresden for their money. Wagner stayed in Dresden for six years, paying off his old bills while incurring newer and larger ones.

In 1845, another of his operas, *Tannhauser,* was performed in Dresden. Wagner's newly found good luck had run out. The audience didn't like the music, and they thought the story was immoral. Tannhauser is a singer who lived a rather bawdy life. During a singing competition, where the prize is marriage to the beautiful Elizabeth, Tannhauser shocks everyone, and forfeits the contest, by singing about physical love, rather than spiritual. In the end, it is Elizabeth's death that saves him. He too dies, but is redeemed by her love (an ending made popular by Goethe's *Faust).*

Tannhauser presented some musical difficulties. Wagner was just beginning to "find himself," to compose in a new style. His strange discords and harmonics not only presented new sounds to the audience, but created difficulties for the singers too.

Though Wagner was making these changes in harmonics and orchestration, both *Tannhäuser* and *Dutchman* were traditional operas. They had a number of arias, duets, choruses, and other traditional opera scenes, including dances. The revolution that Wagner would bring to opera, and to all fields of music, was as yet in its formative stage.

The Exile

During the general political upheavals in France and Germany in 1848, when the people were calling for a new age of equality, Wagner joined forces with the rebels. He wrote antigovernment articles and even gave political speeches. The idea of a New Order in which he might emerge as a leader, rekindled his megalomania. "I will destroy the existing order of things," he trumpeted in his nihilistic pamphlets, publicly denouncing royalty. "Rise up, people, and do away with the kings and queens and let us all be as one." He also called for the abolition of money. "There should be no rich and no poor, no creditors," he wrote. We can well understand his motivation for writing this.

The gamble didn't pay off for Wagner: the revolution failed. This time the payment meant more than debtor's prison. To escape a long jail term, and possibly a death sentence, Wagner fled from Germany.

He stopped at Weimar first to see Franz Liszt. He gave Liszt the manuscript for his opera *Lohengrin.* It is from this opera that we get the famous Wedding March. Like his previous works, Lohengrin, too, is traditional opera, but the new coherence of the arts that Wagner was seeking suggests itself here, where the drama and music create a unified mood. Liszt directed the first performance in 1850. Wagner did not dare attend, for fear the King had sent soldiers to look for him.

Wagner went to Zurich, Switzerland, where he stayed for ten years. He spent his time writing articles about music, beginning his attack on the old forms and styles. He started composing what he referred to as the "Music of the Future." He would create operas that would be more than just beautiful music. "There must be a coming together of all the arts," Wagner wrote. "A synthesis of the art of music, literature, painting, set design, and drama." He began a project, *Der Ring des Nibelungen* (The Ring of the Nibelungs), that would take the next twenty-five years to complete.

In the meantime, Wagner supported himself and Minna by conducting. Even at that he was an original, insisting on his own interpretations about rhythm and dynamics, even when they disagreed with what the composer might have expressly written on the score. He toured those countries where he didn't fear arrest, and even went to London in 1855, earning a substantial sum of money with his conductor's baton. He also received advances from different publishing firms, which helped him get through his financial difficulties.

Though in exile, he was not forgotten. His operas, *Rienzi, Tannhauser,* and *Lohengrin* were constantly performed. "I think I am the only person in Europe," he once complained, "who has yet to see a performance of *Lohengrin.*"

Even in those cities where his operas were not being produced (the Parisians were long unreceptive to Wagner's music), his operas were constantly in people's minds. His new ideas about unifying the arts, especially as he propagated them in his published essays, were being discussed everywhere in the art world. Quite early in his career, Wagner became the most talked about and controversial composer of his time.

Other Exiles

Many artists were caught up in the revolutions that traveled like wildfire over the European continent. Among them was Victor Hugo. Hugo (1802-1885), one of France's greatest writers, was a poet, dramatist, essayist, and novelist. As a playwright, Hugo conscientiously sought to replace the classical dramas with a more vibrant, personal, romantic drama. He wrote mostly historical plays, with an emphasis on character development. In 1827, Hugo attached a preface to his play *Cromwell,* stating his intent to break away from the classical school. "Our new plays should be free in form and subject, not subject to neoclassical rules." He also insisted that the classical idea of unity could be dispensed with. He defended the juxtaposition of tragic and comic scenes. "Life is not all one mood," he declared. "Let us explore all the heights and depths of man's soul."

Hugo was a member of the French Academy, and during the beginning of the 1848 revolution, he sided with Louis Napoleon. But he soon became one of the leaders of the democratic party, calling for greater freedom for the people. When the revolution was defeated, Hugo went into exile. It was during his years in exile that he produced his greatest works, among them the novel *Les Miserables.* His most popular work, *Les Miserables* is a story about a poor man sent to prison for stealing a loaf of bread to feed his family. In the fashion of the romantics, the hero of the story, although a victim of society, is purified and somehow made better by his suffering.

It was also Hugo who created the unforgettable character, the hunchback of Notre Dame, in one of his earlier novels.

Hugo was like Wagner in more ways than one. Besides being an ardent romantic and political activist, he was perhaps the one man in the nineteenth century whose ego could match Wagner's, although the other French writer, Honore de Balzac, was also filled with self-pride. "They are right to idolize me," Hugo said of the French public after his triumphal return to Paris in 1870. "I am the greatest writer who has ever lived." He was so caught up in visions of his own greatness, that he insisted throughout the last years of his life that the capital of France be renamed: instead of "Paris" he wanted it called "Hugo."

Even in his 70s, and until the time of his death, this great writer remained a revolutionary. In his last days, he embraced communism, seeing in that ideology the greatest salvation for the poor of the earth. "There would be no Les Miserables," he said, "if there were no wealthy parasites who were always getting rich at everyone else's expense." He died believing that it was the artist's responsibility to go on fighting against the injustices in society.

The Human Comedy

Wagner wasn't the only nineteenth century artist with grandiose ideas, who wanted to synthesize all the arts. Another great French writer, Honore de Balzac (1799-1850), was filled with ambition. Like Chopin, Balzac preferred the company of aristocrats to any other group. The "de" in his name was something he added on his own, to make it sound more of noble origin.

His pretensions went beyond changing his name. Balzac was a notorious spendthrift, again like Wagner, constantly spending huge sums to live in the grand style. As a result, he was almost always in debt. Because of his debts, he became one of the most prolific of all writers, writing novel after novel in order to earn money.

Balzac is a good example of the literary figures who was always ahead of his time, challenging the conventions of his contemporaries and establishing new artistic forms. Living in the time of the early musical romantics, even socializing with Chopin in the Parisian salons, Balzac was, nevertheless, creating a new art form, going beyond romanticism to bring realism into his novels and stories. While the romantics were depicting medieval and mythological heroes, Balzac was writing about lawyers, bankers, journalists, and doctors, members of the middle classes of his own time. His detailed observations about these characters and their way of life were almost scientific. There is a sense of objectivity and detachment about his work that is quite different from the subjectivity found in romanticism.

Balzac wrote a series of works, called *The Human Comedy*, which comprised almost 100 novels and short stories. It was in this series that he moved ahead of his romantic contemporaries to lay the foundation for the realistic movement. His studies of the human condition, of detailed settings and minute character descriptions, set him apart from other writers. His subjects were usually related to his own personal life, money-making and social climbing. Yet there were many romantic elements in his work: excesses of passion, individualistic characters, and scenes evoking strong emotions. Balzac was not entirely a realist.

In his personal life, Balzac was very much like Wagner and Victor Hugo. He was a strong-willed, passionate person, constantly chasing women, filled with a superabundance of self-pride. While Wagner sought a synthesis of all the arts, Balzac sought no less than a synthesis of all of life. "I am the secretary of society," he said, "seeking to capture the minutes of existence." This "secretary of society" would prove to be as influential a force in literature as Wagner was to be in music. All that is contemporary in music today stems from Wagner; all that is contemporary in literature today, especially the New Journalism, has its roots in the writings of Honore de Balzac.

Tristan and Isolde

While in Zurich, Wagner was befriended by a wealthy Swiss businessman, Otto Wesendonck, who was an admirer of his operas. Wesendonck helped Wagner financially, arranging for performances of his work and allowing all the proceeds to go to the composer. In 1857, he saw to it that the Wagners were situated comfortably, and rent-free, in a house on his estate.

Wagner repaid his new friend by seducing his wife. He and the beautiful Mathilde Wesendonck began an open love affair that was the talk of Zurich, humiliating both Otto and Minna, who did their best to ignore it. Wagner had done the same thing a few years previously while visiting Paris. Monsieur Laussot, a wine merchant and admirer of opera, offered Wagner the hospitality of his home for several weeks. Wagner accepted and then tried to convince Laussot's wife to run off with him. She almost did.

There was one good thing that came from Wagner's overworked libido. His beautiful opera, *Tristan and Isolde,* was inspired by his affair with Mathilde.

Tristan and Isolde has been acclaimed as the most beautiful and stirring expression of love ever presented on the musical stage. Tristan is a knight sent to Ireland to escort the lovely Isolde back to England to King Mark. Because of a love potion they drink, Tristan and Isolde fall in love and betray the king. When they are discovered, Tristan is killed in a duel, and Isolde, heartbroken, follows him in death.

Wagner used the *leitmotif* as the unifying element of the opera. His melody is allowed to flow without pause, filling every movement of the opera with intense sound. The heavy use of chromaticism and unusual harmonic progressions makes *Tristan and Isolde,* not only one of the most unique operas composed in the romantic period, but one of the most difficult for musicians and singers to perform. The first attempt at producing this opera, in Vienna in 1861, was abandoned when the musicians and singers, *after fifty-four rehearsals(!),* gave up in disgust. Here are the opening measures of the opera, which show Wagner's unorthodox approach to traditional tonality:

Wagner also interrupted his work on the *Ring* cycle (the *Ring of the Nibelungs* project had grown to four separate operas) to compose *The Mastersinger of Nuremberg.* Like his earlier opera *Tannhauser, The Mastersinger* is about a young man who enters a singing contest to win the hand of the woman he loves. *The Mastersinger* is Wagner's only comedy. He returned to the traditional style in this opera, using arias, duets, chorals, and dances. The fine story and lyrical music have made more than one opera lover wish he had composed more in this vein. The Overture is especially lively and colorful; it is often excerpted as a concert piece.

His exile was a very productive period, but when amnesty was finally granted in 1860, Wagner was overjoyed to be able to return to his homeland.

An Open Wallet

Wagner still had to go on conducting tours around Europe and Russia to earn a living. After 1862 he only had to earn enough for himself. Minna had left him, unable to put up with his continued infidelity and selfish behavior.

In 1864, Wagner finally got the kind of recognition he was seeking. The King of Bavaria, young Ludwig II, publicly acclaimed Wagner's greatness and promised to subsidize all the composer's works. He paid off Wagner's enormous debts, set the composer up in regal style in Munich, and underwrote the production of all Wagner's new compositions. He did this out of feelings of love and respect for Wagner and his works, not in an offhand royal gesture of largesse. Wagner represented the German spirit in his music, and Ludwig, an ardent nationalist, felt it the duty of the German state to support that music.

With the royal treasury at his disposal, Wagner's extravagances bordered on the ridiculous. He had the walls of his apartment covered with expensive leather, imported valuable vases from China, and had large tapestries depicting his operas handmade to his order.

During the four years that he enjoyed the king's protection, he had *Tristan and Isolde* and *The Mastersinger* premiered in Munich. He also was able to spend a great deal of time composing the music for the first two operas in the *Ring* cycle.

Wagner's adversities were far from over. Despite the king's friendship, almost everybody else of importance in Munich disliked the egocentric composer. The music critics and other artists were hostile to his work and his general idea of combining all the arts into one grand spectacular; and the politicians were jealous of his intimacy with the king. Wagner's every step was watched, and every misstep was used by the gossips as another wedge to place between Wagner and King Ludwig. What bothered the townsfolk most though, and gave them the most to talk about, was Wagner's new love affair. Once more Wagner was involved with somebody else's wife.

Cosima

Cosima was the daughter of Franz Liszt, born out of wedlock to Liszt and the Countess D'Agoult.

She was a remarkable woman, the first woman Wagner had met who could, not only give him the full appreciation he constantly needed, but who could actually understand what his work was all about.

Her husband, Hans von Bulow, was a concert pianist. He was one of the first virtuosos to devote his talents mainly to performing, rather than to composing. He was well known for his interpretations of Chopin, Mendelssohn, and Liszt, and he was a fervent admirer of Richard Wagner. He considered it quite an honor when Wagner offered him his friendship, not realizing who it was Wagner really wanted to be friendly with.

When Wagner was called to Munich by King Ludwig, he arranged to have von Bulow appointed court pianist, just to keep Cosima close to him. Had Hans refused the appointment, Cosima would have gone to Munich without him.

This affair, openly conducted and even brazenly flaunted before the townsfolk and the unhappy husband, led to Wagner's dismissal from Munich. In 1868, Wagner and Cosima, with *their* two children, declared that they were moving to Switzerland. Von Bulow did not try to stop them.

In 1870, after Cosima's divorce and Minna's death, Cosima and Wagner were able to get married. Wagner promised her that he would never be unfaithful again. He did not keep the promise.

The Ring of the Nibelungs: One Man's Monument

It took Wagner twenty-five years to complete the story and music for his four-part music drama, *The Ring of the Nibelungs.* It takes four evenings to see the entire cycle performed. It is undoubtedly the most monumental achievement in music.

Wagner did not intend to write such a gigantic opera. He began with the story of the death of Siegfried, but finding that incomplete, started working backward and composed the other three operas. The operas are titled *The Rhine Gold, The Valkyries, Siegfried,* and *The Twilight of the Gods.*

He took the stories from German and Scandinavian legends of the twelfth century. The main theme of the legend is that man, through lust and greed and the failure to love, destroys himself and everything around him.

Consistent with his large-scale goals, Wagner greatly enlarged the orchestra of his music drama, especially the brass and wind sections. He even invented a special brass instrument called the Wagner tuba, a cross between a tuba and a French horn. In one part of *The Rhine Gold* he even uses large blacksmith anvils on which a "forging song" is hammered out.

Wagner used the *leitmotif* extensively in the *Ring* cycle. He composed melodic themes for each character, and even for their horses. Siegfried's sword has a theme of its own, and so does a dragon that was slain by the sword. There are hundreds of these separate motifs composed which, interwoven, make up the fabric of the music.

There are no arias or duets in the traditional style. The singing is in the Wagnerian *Sprechsingen* (speech-song) style. The melody flows "endlessly" through the four operas, and the harmony, without the usual resolution of chords, also seems "endless." There are very few special sections of music that call attention to themselves; the music is constantly kept tied to the drama.

The language of the libretto, which took five years in itself to write, is also made as musical as possible. In order to capture the true sound of medieval ballads, Wagner used *Stabreim,* in which internal and external alliteration is employed quite extensively. Alliteration means a repetition of initial sound from one word to another. Here is an example of Wagner's *Stabreim:*

> Bluhenden Lebens, labendes Blut,
> Traufelt Ich in den Trank.
> Bruderbrunstig mutig gemischt,
> Bluh im Trank unser Blut!

Old English folk tales and legends also used heavy alliteration. Here is an example from Beowulf, written more than a 1000 years ago:

> Then from the moorland, by misty crags,
> With God's wrath laden, Grendel came.
> The monster was minded of mankind now
> Sundry to seize in the stately house.

The Story

The story of the *Ring* cycle is very complicated. A magic ring is forged from gold taken from the Rhine river. Whoever possesses the ring is master of the world. Alberich, a member of the Nibelungs, a race of dwarfs that live beneath the earth, has possession of the ring. Wotan, the God of Valhalla, manages to get the ring and all of Alberich's gold. The dwarf curses the god and anyone else who touches the ring.

The ring falls into the hands of the giant-magician Fafner, who turns himself into a dragon to guard it. Wotan realizes that only a human can cope with Fafner, so he goes to earth and fathers twins, Siegmund and Sieglinde.

The twins are separated when they are very young and do not meet again until much later. They fall in love, not knowing they are brother and sister.

Siegmund is killed by the angry Wotan, but Sieglinde escapes with the help of Brünnhilde, Wotan's other daughter. Brünnhilde is punished by being put into a deep sleep and surrounded by a ring of fire.

Siegfried, the son of Siegmund, is born to Sieglinde. He is raised by the dwarf Mime. It is Siegfried who slays the dragon (the giant Fafner) and captures the magic ring. He then rescues Brünnhilde from the fire and, with his kiss, restores her back to life.

Siegfried leaves Brünnhilde to go off in search of adventure. He visits the castle of Gunther, where he is given a potion that robs him of his memory. He is then persuaded to give up Brünnhilde to Gunther, which he does, to Brünnhilde's bitter anger. Not knowing Siegfried has been drugged, she plots to kill him. Siegfried is stabbed in the back by Gunther's halfbrother. Too late, Brünnhilde finds out that Siegfried had been drugged when he betrayed her. Vowing to accompany Siegfried on his journey into death, she mounts her horse and rides directly into the funeral pyre that holds Siegfried's body. The evil halfbrother of Gunther is drowned in the Rhine river, trying to get his hands on the magic ring. With the death of Siegfried and Brünnhilde, who were the offspring of the god Wotan, Valhalla can no longer exist and goes up in a blaze of fire, turning the heavens and the entire world into a holocaust.

The Bayreuth Festival

Wagner knew that his *Ring* cycle would make tremendous demands not only on the audience, but on the singers and musicians. He dreamed of a special theater for the presentation of his works that would have the best acoustics possible; where the seating would be such that everyone in the theater could have an excellent view of the stage; where the orchestra would be out of sight and not distract from the action on stage; and where the stage itself would house the very latest in theater technology.

Around 1870 Wagner decided that there would be such a theater built just for his works. "It is not enough to create such a monumental cycle," he told Cosima. "I must also bring into existence a new theater, a temple, where my music can be properly performed."

For a man who had spent time in jail for nonpayment of debt, Wagner certainly had grandiose ideas. Building the theater he imagined would take hundreds of thousands of dollars. But it was his goal, and nothing could stop him once he set his mind on something. He sought out patrons, gave innumerable concerts to collect money, and even set up special Wagner societies in order to fund his project.

In 1872, in Bayreuth, Germany, the building actually began. King Ludwig eventually supplied most of the money for the theater to be completed. In 1876, on August 13th, the first complete performance of *The Ring of the Nibelungens* began. The Bayreuth Festival lasted for five days. It was the culmination of the most ambitious artistic undertaking since the days of the Renaissance. Musicians from all over the world attended, including such greats as Liszt and Tchaikovsky. There were over 4000 visitors at Bayreuth, including scores of newspaper reporters from every country imaginable. All the royalty of Europe attended, dukes, princes, and even emperors, paying homage to the man who once called for their destruction.

Every Year, Wagner

Wagner lost money on the opening of his theater in 1876 and had to wait until 1882 before he could present a second cycle. He composed one last opera, *Parsifal,* which was restricted to performances at Bayreuth only for thirty years. That would help attract more people to the annual festival. It was first presented in 1882, during the second festival.

After that, Wagner went to Venice to rest. The years of labor had taxed his strength. It would be a long rest. On February 13, 1883, he suffered a heart attack and suddenly died. His body was carried back to Bayreuth where he was given a hero's burial.

The theater in Bayreuth went on, though. Wagner festivals were held by Cosima and then by the Wagner children. Today Wieland Wagner, one of the grandsons, is carrying on at Bayreuth, and the Wagner Festival is still one of the high points of a European trip.

The Legacy

Wagner appealed to that part of the romantic's psyche that craved the heroic and the mystical. His operas revived the glory of the medieval past and offered the public grand heroes and heroines.

His extreme use of dissonance, though, and his minimizing of the upper melodic line led to serious changes in music. To get an "endless flow of music," Wagner gave a greater importance to the lower harmonic line, while the upper vocal line was kept in check. This helped mark an end to a period that prided itself on its soaring melodies and individual songs.

Wagner's heavy use of dissonance, which underscored the longing of the romantic era, signaled the start, for better or worse, of an entirely new concept of music, the atonal system. As far as "progress" in music was concerned, Wagner had tested the very limits of th tonal system, and left very little for the composers who came after him to explore or develop. Except for a brief period of impressionism, post-Wagnerian music has meant atonal music: discordant, disconnected sounds that mock the very essence of what music meant to the great composers of the past. It is a very dubious legacy that Richard Wagner left, one that even he would find difficult to appreciate.

Study Activities

1. Read the scenes and listen to the following selections from Wagner's *Ring*. How well does the music serve the drama?

    "Ride of the Valkyries" from Act III *The Valkyries*.
    "Forest Murmers" from Act II *Siegfried*.
    "Siegfried's Death and Funeral Music," from Act III *The Twilight of the Gods*.

2. The influence of Wagner's philosophical writings and music on Adolf Hitler is documented in William Shirer's book *The Rise and Fall of the Third Reich* (in Chapter 4, "The Mind of Hitler and the Roots of the Third Reich"). Read that chapter and discuss this unusual relationship between a composer and the Second World War.

3. There have been many books written about the symbolic meaning of *The Ring of the Nibelungs*. Here are two:

    Donington, R. *Wagner's Ring and its Symbols*. New York, 1963.
    Gutman, R. *Richard Wagner: The Man, His Mind, and His Music*. New York, 1968.

    Using the above books and others, compile a list of the symbols and their meanings in Wagner's work. Then discuss the purpose of these symbols and their effectiveness in a work of art.

4. Wagner was a great composer and gave the world beautiful music, but he was terrible when it came to personal relationships. He took all he could from others, believing that his genius gave him that right. What do you think about that? Do artists or any other group have a special status in society? Must "ordinary" people make allowances for the "geniuses" among them?

5. Carl Maria von Weber (1786-1826) composed an opera called *Der Freischutz* in 1821. Do some library research on this opera to determine the influence that it had on Wagner.

6. Read one of Balzac's novels, preferably *Pere Goriot* (Father Goriot) or *Eugenie Grandet*. Make a class report on 1) the plot of the story; 2) the different characters; 3) the description of scenes and settings; or 4) how helpful the story is in learning about human relationships.

VIII

Johannes Brahms:

Love Songs and Lullabies

Johannes Brahms was born in 1833 and experienced what was probably the most difficult childhood of any composer since Beethoven. His father was a musician for the Hamburg Opera, but he didn't earn enough money to support his family. Often, the Brahms family went hungry.

When Johannes exhibited a talent for music, his father encouraged him and even paid out precious money for a piano teacher. He expected his son to repay him, however, and at the age of eight, the young boy was sent out to earn money playing the piano in the taverns on the waterfront, the toughest district of Hamburg. His payment was a few dollars a night and all the beer he could drink. The many unsavory characters he met and had to contend with during those years left an impression on him that would last for life.

Brahms

When he was ten, Brahms found a new teacher, Eduard Marxsen, who was to be his friend for the next forty years. Under Marxsen's guidance, Brahms' playing was perfected, and he even began to do some composing.

Brahms had to work hard to support himself and to contribute to his family's support. Through his teen years he worked for different publishers, arranging other composers' work and supplying the publishers with hack compositions of his own.

At the age of twenty, Brahms had the good fortune to team up with the Hungarian violinist Remenyi, who had heard him playing in one of the taverns. Remenyi gave concerts all over the world, and for a year, Brahms toured Europe with him. Accompanying the Hungarian violinist acquainted Brahms with the Hungarian melodies and rhythms that he would later use in his own compositions.

The playing experience he got on tour with Remenyi was not half as important as the contacts he made with other professionals in the music world. Most important was his meeting with the violinist Joseph Joachim, a very influential musician. It was through Joachim that Brahms met Franz Liszt, who gave the young composer important encouragement; and it was also to Joachim's credit that Brahms met Robert Schumann, the composer whom Brahms admired second only to Beethoven.

First Friends, First Love

When Brahms first visited Robert and Clara Schumann, it was with some trepidation. Schumann was his idol, and it seemed like a dream come true to be in his living room playing the piano for him. His nervousness increased when he saw how distant and cold Schumann appeared. He did not know of Schumann's illness. "Go ahead and play," he was told.

Brahms had chosen one of his recent compositions to play for Schumann and began sounding the notes of his *Sonata in C Major*. Within seconds the ice had melted. "My word," breathed Schumann, "you're a genius."

Schumann's generosity did not stop at verbal compliments and encouragement. For the next three months, the Schumanns kept Brahms with them. Robert immediately wrote an article for his *New Journal of Music,* describing Brahms as one of the greatest artists to recently appear on the scene. He also introduced the fledgling composer to the publishing firm of Breitkopf and Hartel, who agreed to publish some of Brahms' compositions. Clara included his works at her popular recitals and did her best to make the public aware of this new young composer.

The friendship would last for the rest of their lives. Unhappily, Robert was not to live much longer. Within a year, he would go insane and have to be confined to an asylum.

Brahms was in Hamburg when he heard about Schumann's mental breakdown. He hurried back to Dusseldorf to be with Clara. For the next two years he devoted himself to helping her, being her companion, assisting with the children, and accompanying her to the asylum to visit Robert. Without realizing it, he was falling in love with her.

After Schumann's death, Brahms became the music director for the Prince of Lippe-Detmold, about 100 miles from Dusseldorf. His move away from Clara, though he loved her fervently, was typical of his actions regarding women. He could fall in love with them (he did so rather frequently), but he could never bring himself to share his life with anyone. He could never get over the unhappy childhood he had experienced. His own parents were constantly at each other's throats because of money, and the sad procession of broken men and women he had seen in the taverns on the waterfront had left traumatic scars. Brahms remained a bachelor all his life, a solitary figure who liked people but kept them at a safe distance.

The Struggle Upward

Brahms worked in several German cities during the next few years as the choirmaster or music director of small inconsequential groups. He went to Hanover in 1859 to introduce his first major orchestral work, his *Piano Concerto No. 1*. Joachim conducted the orchestra, and Brahms was at the piano. It was not a success.

Brahms was to have a lot of trouble getting this concerto accepted. When it was first performed, the audiences complained that it was too long and unnecessarily moody. Subsequent performances failed to change their minds. The concerto seemed too intense, even elegiac (it was composed shortly after Robert Schumann's death). Piano concertos were noted for their brilliance and lyricism. It took some time before the austerity of Brahms' work made a positive impression.

His second concerto for piano and orchestra is epic in structure, much like his first symphony. There are four movements instead of three. It is filled with beautiful melodies, more in keeping with his audience's expectations. The lyrical cello solo in the beginning of the third movement is taken from one of Brahms' own songs. The melody is shared by the other members of the orchestra, before it is taken over by the piano and fully developed. The final movement is filled with Hungarian melodies and rhythms, reminiscences of his friend Remenyi.

In 1859, Brahms was working in Hamburg as a choirmaster. He stayed there for four years, making occasional visits to Vienna. He made good friends on those visits to Vienna, and some of his work was premiered down there. He was still having a difficult time getting the public to like his compositions. They neither had the light touch of Mendelssohn, the brilliance of Liszt, nor the soul-stirring emotionalism of Chopin.

"Let us not give up," his friend Joseph Hellmesberger told him. Hellmesberger was one of the leaders in the musical world of Vienna. He led another concert of Brahms' works, this time including the *Piano Quartet in A Major* and the now popular *Variations on a Theme by Handel*. Brahms himself played the piano. This time the audience responded favorably. It was a beginning.

When Brahms could not get the position he wanted as director of the Philharmonic Society in Hamburg, he decided to move permanently to Vienna, the one place where his music had been appreciated. It was a wise decision.

In Praise of Death

Brahms worked as a conductor in Vienna, earning his keep while working on his compositions. Brahms was thirty-five years old before he achieved the success he was seeking. He made his mark with a religious choral work, *The German Requiem*. Unlike most requiems (music commemorating death), Brahms' work is not sorrowful. It is highly emotional, emphasizing man's search for truth and understanding and his longing to know what awaits him after life. It is not music of despair or fear. "Death is not a eternal annihilation; it leads us to a better, more contented and fulfilled existence." These words in the text, matched by the soaring, optimistic music, moved his audience to thunderous applause. This religious hymn finally gave Brahms the standing he wanted in musical Vienna (paradoxically, Brahms was a free thinker and rather irreligious; it is doubtful that he believed one single word in the entire *Requiem*).

In 1873, Brahms was considered the finest conductor and composer in Vienna. His orchestral *Variations on a Theme by Haydn* won immediate acclaim, and a number of people began comparing him to Beethoven.

The *Variations* was composed originally as a duet for piano, and was first performed by Clara Schumann and Brahms in 1873. The piece was then orchestrated a few months later, and it became the first set of orchestral variations to be presented as an independent composition. One usually found orchestral variations of this nature as a movement within a larger work, not as a work by itself. As variations had long been independent works for the piano and violin, Brahms saw no reason why they couldn't be symphonic as well. He was right. His *Variations* pleased both the critics and the public.

The theme was from one of Haydn's minor works, suggested to Brahms by Haydn's biographer, C. F. Pohle. The theme is introduced by the wind and string instruments. It is then repeated in eight separate variations, first by the strings, then by the clarinets, next by the oboes, and so on, until the entire orchestra takes up the final version in a fittingly dramatic outburst. The third variation, marked *con moto* (with animation), is an especially lyrical episode presented in the oboes and strings; the fourth variation, with its two melodic ideas presented simultaneously, is reminiscent of Tchaikovsky's sensuous music; and the finale is a passacaglia: here Brahms presents variations (the passacaglia) upon variations (the Haydn theme), a rather ingenious ending which the audience didn't fail to notice and appreciate.

Chamber Works

Brahms liked to use other baroque forms besides the passacaglia, such as the concerto grosso, fugues, and sonatas. While many of the Wagnerians considered him "backward" because of this, Brahms actually helped spark the revival of baroque music and forms that many twentieth century composers have gotten involved in.

In keeping with his interest in baroque and classical forms, Brahms wrote an astonishing variety of chamber works. He composed piano quartets, string quartets and quintets, string sextets, clarinet quintets, clarinet trios, piano trios, violin trios, cello trios, and combinations, such as for the clarinet and piano, violin and piano, and cello and piano. There was almost no end to them.

These works show a variety of moods: graceful adagios, lively waltzes, and vibrant gypsy rhythms and melodies. His *String Quintet in G Major* is, by itself, a study in contrasting moods. The first movement is a forceful duet of cello and violins which breaks out toward the end into a Strauss-like waltz; the next movement is a melancholy adagio, with the violins dominant; the following scherzo reintroduces the waltz, restoring the more cheerful mood of the first movement; and the finale ends with one of those Hungarian gypsy dances for which Brahms is famous.

Like his good friend and benefactor Robert Schumann, Brahms was also a creator of German lieder (songs), which were rivaling orchestral chamber works. One of Brahms' songs is possibly the best known melody in the world, and the very first song many of us ever hear: "Wiegenlied" (Cradle-song), otherwise known as "The Brahms Lullaby."

An Enemy of Progress

Brahms was of course a romantic. He wanted his music to be as expressive of his emotions as possible. He did not belong to the school that stemmed from Chopin and found its greatest expression in Liszt and Wagner. Instead, he had classical leanings very much like Mendelssohn. He preferred to place his music in traditional forms.

He did not like program music. Brahms did not believe in linking his music to a story or to metaphysics. "Music should be pure, a thing true to itself."

Throughout the nineteenth century, there was a constant conflict between these two groups. In the 1860s, Brahms and others of the school of "pure" music signed a proclamation denouncing Wagner and the "Music of the Future." Liszt was, of course, on the side of Wagner and he too, with his philosophy of free forms, romantic exuberance, and the association of music with all the arts, was denounced. The Brahms group wanted to return to classical principles and checkmate what they considered musical excesses. As for the Wagnerians, they considered Brahms dull and backward, an enemy of progress.

But Brahms was not so easily categorized. He had very unpredictable tastes. He didn't like Wagner's operas, but then he didn't care for Verdi's either, supposedly the opposite of the Wagner style. He also wrote off Tchaikovsky, whose beautiful symphonies were composed along classical lines. He did, however, like Dvorak and Grieg, not only because his own tastes for Hungarian and North German songs were shared by these two men, but also because he admired their nationalistic tendencies, which were among Wagner's strongest traits as well. He greatly admired Johann Strauss, whose waltzes were considered "popular music." Frau Strauss once asked Brahms to autograph her fan. He quickly sketched the opening notes of her husband's *Blue Danube Waltz* and wrote beneath the notes, "Alas, not by Johannes Brahms."

Out of Step With Time

The closest counterpart to Brahms in the literary world was the English poet and critic Matthew Arnold (1822-88). Arnold was the son of a teacher; he would become a teacher and administrator of schools himself.

Like Brahms, Arnold, too, was anachronistic, seeking to reestablish classical precepts in a romantic age. The greatest virtues a writer could possess, he claimed, were "clearness of arrangement, rigor of development, and simplicity of style." He believed an artist should be objective rather than subjective, expressing ideas rather than portraying emotions.

Like Brahms, Arnold was also a free thinker. To him, the Bible was little more than a collection of lovely poems and inspiring stories. He sought to answer the questions of existence for himself: why are we here; where is man heading; what are the best values to have. The answers he came up with were not very pleasant. He was one of the first thinkers to view life existentially, to see life as absurd and to realize that each human being exists in a state of isolation from all others and from everything else around him. His most famous poem, *Dover Beach*, best shows this aspect of Arnold's philosophy. Here are some parts from that poem:

The sea is calm to-night.
The tide is full, the moon lies fair
Upon the straits. . .

Listen! you hear the grating roar
Of pebbles which the waves draw back, and fling,
At their return, up the high strand,
Begin, and cease, and then again begin,
With tremulous cadence slow, and bring
The eternal note of sadness in. . .

Ah, love, let us be true
To one another! for the world, which seems
To lie before us like a land of dreams,
So various, so beautiful, so new,
Hath really neither joy, nor love, nor light,
Nor certitude, nor peace, nor help for pain;
And we are here as on a darkling plain
Swept with confused alarms of struggle and flight
Where ignorant armies clash by night.

Arnold followed the classical ideals of restraint, lucidity, and balance when writing poetry, which is quite obvious in the above excerpt. He also, again like Brahms, infused a melancholy into his work that gave the work its own special depth of expression, which was quite romantic and in keeping with the temper of the times. While the form of his work is classical, the content, which depicts isolation from a society that is caught up in confusion and chaos, is unmistakably romantic.

A Hard Act to Follow

Brahms usually composed in sets of two: two quartets, two serenades, two overtures, two sextets. Even his symphonies were composed that way, his *First* and *Second* in 1876 and 1877, his *Third* and *Fourth* in 1883 and 1884.

Brahms was over forty when his *First Symphony* was produced. He wanted to be sure he was mature enough to undertake such a project; he knew that most composers' first symphonies were usually forgotten soon after they were composed, including the great Mozart's, Schubert's, and even Beethoven's first symphony. He didn't want that to happen to him.

He was hesitant to write a symphony for another reason. "How can anyone write a symphony today," he once remarked, "when we hear the giant footsteps of Beethoven behind us? Who can compete with him?"

Finally in 1876, after years of working on it, Brahms completed his *Symphony No. 1*. It was an epic work. The movements were so large that his symphony was twice as long as one by Haydn or Mozart.

Despite its beautiful opening and sustained lyricism, the symphony did not have the effect on the public that he had expected. It received a mixed reaction, and Brahms was deeply disappointed. He went right to work on another symphony. That one, too, the *Second Symphony*, composed within a year of the first, failed to please the critics. It was a pastoral symphony, reflecting the lovely Austrian village where Brahms had first conceived the idea for it. It was completely different from the preceding symphony with its dark and melancholy tone, but still it received mixed reviews. Some thought he emulated Beethoven too much in his *First Symphony,* and others thought his *Second Symphony* was too superficial.

Still Brahms tried; he wrote two more symphonies. Of those, only his *Third Symphony* received the type of applause he had anticipated, and mostly because of the intensely beautiful third and fourth movements.

The *Third Symphony* was not composed until six years after the *Second.* When it was first performed, a clique of Wagnerians were in the audience to hiss and boo, and they almost caused a riot. Fortunately, the majority of the audience overwhelmed the hecklers with their applause. The symphony was obviously a success. The audience especially liked the third movement, which held one of the most melodic orchestral songs ever composed (the great tenor Mario Lanza made it famous as a hit song in the early 1950s).

The Wagnerians tried to cause trouble for Brahms because they believed that the symphonic form was obsolete. Their heroes, like Liszt, wrote tone poems rather than symphonies, or like Wagner, avoided orchestral scores as an exclusive form and concentrated on music dramas, which linked the orchestra to the other arts. Although it took some time for his symphonies to win over the public at large, and they finally did, Brahms proved them wrong (as Tchaikovsky would do): classical forms were far from obsolete.

Still the Master

Brahms was having some difficulty with his symphonies, but that did not mean he was losing his status as the foremost composer in Vienna and one of the greatest in the world. On the contrary, during the 1870s and 80s, Brahms composed many works, most of them masterpieces in their own form, such as the compositions for clarinet, the Trio, Quintet and Sonata. It was also during this period that he composed one of his greatest works, his violin concerto.

The *Violin Concerto in D Major* was composed in 1878 in his summer place in Portschach near the Austrian-Yugoslav border. The pastoral setting had a very beneficial effect on Brahms. During each of the three summers he stayed there he produced a masterpiece, a symphony, the violin concerto, and a piano concerto.

Brahms composed the violin concerto for his friend Joachim. He collaborated with the violinist on the solo part, seeking Joachim's advice and, after many fierce arguments, revising the violin section as Joachim suggested.

The very long orchestral introduction that begins the concerto (a hundred measures) indicates what is to come, not only in themes, but in length. The concerto is quite long, requiring forty minutes to be performed. The last two movements are the most stirring, capable of competing with the great violin concertos of Mendelssohn and Tchaikovsky. The second movement of the concerto has two sensitive and melancholy melodies that go right to the heart of the audience. The third movement contains another of Brahms' fascinating Hungarian dances; the soloist double-stops the violin (producing two or more simultaneous notes with the bow), giving the impression that he is being accompanied by some invisible violinist standing beside him. It is quite a virtuoso effect, matching the overall artistry of the entire concerto.

Filling Beethoven's Shoes

In many ways, personal as well as professional, Brahms was like Beethoven. He was a bachelor all his life; he received much of his inspiration from the same countryside surrounding Vienna; and he was even as difficult to get along with. They also looked alike, except for Brahms' beard. They were both short and stocky and utterly careless about their appearance. In fact, Brahms was downright sloppy, living in the clutter of a three-room apartment that overflowed with books and music and screamed for a good spring-cleaning. He also wore the same baggy trousers and wrinkled coat day in and day out. It is amazing that such well-ordered and even meticulous compositions came from such an absent-minded person.

Musically, both men had a lot in common. Beethoven was a classicist, looking forward to the new age of romanticism and adjusting his art to include romantic expression. Brahms was a romantic, a man of great depth and feeling, who looked backward in time to link his art to the traditions of the classical age. He wanted his music to express his profound feelings about life, but he believed in shaping and refining those feelings by using classical forms. Brahms' aim was truly romantic; he used form to intensify the emotional content, not to restrain it. He followed Beethoven who expanded form to accommodate his expressive music, but who never departed wholly from the basic patterns of Mozart and Haydn.

He was also just as unpredictable, musically, as Beethoven. In 1881, the University of Breslau awarded Brahms an honary Doctorate. Brahms composed an overture, *The Academic Festival Overture,* for the occasion. Such serious activities called for solemn music, but, to everybody's surprise and delight, the mercurial Brahms had composed a lively work based on several cheerful college drinking songs, all easily identified in the *Overture.*

His good spirits, more often than not, were cloaked by a gruff exterior. Brahms was very direct with everyone, speaking his mind candidly, and occasionally (again like Beethoven) without tact. He grew more blunt in his later years, but most people understood him and accepted his shocking honesty without taking offense. His was a familiar figure around Vienna, walking with his hands behind his back, his head bowed forward in deep thought, and a melody occasionally breaking forth from his lips, as he worked out a new section in his latest composition.

Sadly, in the beginning of 1897, Brahms discovered that he had cancer. Within a few months, his body grew thin, and he aged considerably. When he died on April 3rd, it was a day of mourning for everyone. He was buried next to Beethoven, the music from his own *Requiem* giving some comfort to his mourners.

Study Activities

1. Anton Dvorak, a friend of Brahms, came to the United States in 1892 and directed the National Music School for two years. While here, he composed his famous *Symphony No. 9* which he subtitled "From the New World." Listen to the symphony. What familiar melodies do you hear? Does folk music often find its way into symphonic literature? What composers in both the classical and romantic periods brought folk music into their compositions?

2. Edvard Grieg, another of Brahms' friends, was the national composer of Norway, putting countless Norwegian folk songs into his symphonic suites. Write a brief paper or prepare a class report on Grieg's life and music.

3. What folk song or contemporary popular song do you believe would make a good major theme for a symphony? How would you expand that two or three minute song into a fifteen minute first movement?

4. Brahms and Liszt argued over the use of form. That argument goes on today in most fields of modern art. To what extent can art be "formless"? Is anything entirely without form?

5. The early romantic poets, with the exception of Byron, were transcendentalists. Toward the end of the century, poets tended to be existentialists. Do some library research on these two philosophies. How do they differ in their understanding of man's relationship to 1) himself, 2) society, 3) nature, 4) God?

IX

Giuseppe Verdi:

The Voice of Freedom

Verdi was born in 1813, the same year as Wagner, in a small village in northern Italy. He showed an early talent for music, playing on an old spinet his father, a local grocer, bought for him. The church organist offered to give the boy lessons, and soon young Verdi was able to act as his assistant.

When he was twelve, Verdi was sent to the nearby town of Busseto where he studied with the organist there. He impressed the towns-folk so much with his playing that they organized a fund to send him to the city of Milan to study at the famous Conservatory.

Verdi was eighteen when he went to Milan, and he discovered that he was too old to enter the Conservatory. Even if he had gotten there a few years sooner, they would have turned him down: he failed to pass the entrance exam. "You just don't have enough musical talent," the director told him, never dreaming he was talking to the person who would become the most famous opera composer in the whole world and *remain* the most famous.

Verdi

Deeply disappointed, Verdi returned to Busetto and accepted a position as the director of the local music school. He married Margherita Barezzi, whom he had loved for many years, and for the next four years, he worked hard at his teaching duties and at composing.

There were few opportunities in Busseto, so Verdi and Margherita moved to Milan. The young couple had many financial struggles, but they managed to be happy despite them. Milan was a big city, and they explored it like children, delighting in the many shops and theaters, even though they could seldom afford to buy anything or go to any of the concerts or operas. When they started having children of their own, their happiness was further increased. Even when Margherita had to sell her few pieces of jewelry to raise some money, she managed to laugh at their troubles. She had the greatest confidence in her husband and wasn't ashamed to be poor. Such love and strength gave Verdi all the inspiration and encouragement he needed to continue his work. Finally, after many struggles, Verdi's first opera, *Oberto,* was accepted by La Scala, the most famous opera house in Italy. The opera was a success.

The Tragic and the Comic

The director of La Scala, Bartelo Merelli, was the first to recognize Verdi's talent; he agreed not only to produce *Oberto,* but to commission three more operas from Verdi, to be delivered within eight months of each other. He asked Verdi to compose a comic opera next.

While Verdi was working on *A King for a Day,* his infant son got sick. His young daughter had died just a few months before, and the Verdis were in despair when the boy became ill. Margherita bathed him in cool water to fight the very high fever that was raging in his body, but her baby died in her arms. It was a tragic time for her and Verdi. A few months later, Margherita herself became sick. She, too, had a high fever, and Verdi had to watch helplessly as his beloved wife died before his eyes.

Verdi went ahead with his opera as a tribute to Margherita; she had always been the one to encourage him to go on. But, of course, the opera failed. Under such conditions, no man could have composed anything comic.

When Verdi heard the boos and hisses from the audience on opening night, it was as if they were mocking the spirit of his dead wife rather than booing at the opera. It was a bitter experience that changed Verdi's whole attitude about his art and the public. He decided not to compose any more music. "They have no feeling for a man's suffering," he said of the public. "I will never try to please them again."

The Song of Freedom

Several months passed, time spent in mourning his lost wife and children. Then Merelli persuaded Verdi to try again. "It is your profession," said Merelli. "You need not do it to please anyone; just merely to work in your profession."

He did try again. This time he succeeded. In 1842, his opera, *Nabucco,* created a tremendous sensation. Overnight, Verdi became Italy's most popular composer. In *Nabucco,* Verdi introduced a more forceful and rapid style of opera, making both the music and drama move at a dynamic pace; Verdi also enlarged the orchestra, creating more tonal color.

Nabucco was popular because of its spectacular scenes, with their pageantry of colors and motion that filled the stage. It was also popular for another reason. Verdi included political thrusts in his work. In one scene, the Jewish exiles sing "Va, pensiero," a song which expresses their longing for freedom and to return to their homeland. The Italians, under Austrian rule, readily took up this song; before long it was being sung throughout Italy as a symbol of the Italian's defiance of Austria.

A Trilogy of Masterworks

For the next several years, Verdi composed a dozen more operas, most of which were popular. He accepted the fame that came to him with a nonchalance never before, or since, equalled by an artist. It just didn't mean that much to him.

Verdi became an international composer for the first time with his opera *Ernani.* He was thirty-two years old. Verdi went to Paris to supervise a production there, and in 1845, it was playing in London; two years later it played in New York.

Verdi was almost forty years old before he produced his first masterpiece, *Rigoletto.* It had its premiere in 1851. The plot of this opera is like most Italian operas of this period, complicated and melodramatic. Rigoletto, the character for whom the opera is named, is a hunchbacked court jester. He sends his beautiful daughter to the country to keep her from coming in contact with the corrupt court. The Duke comes across Gilda in the country, and they fall in love. She is brought to the court against her father's wishes. Rigoletto hires an assassin to kill the Duke. The killer, not wanting to place himself in jeopardy, kills the first person he sees and presents the body to Rigoletto in a sack. "Here is the Duke," the killer tells him, collecting his payment and fleeing. Rigoletto takes the sack to the river and is about to throw it in, when he hears the Duke singing in the distance. He quickly opens the sack and finds that his hired assassin had murdered his own daughter, Gilda.

Two of the arias from *Rigoletto* are frequently sung in recitals, apart from the opera. One of them, "La donna e mobile" (the woman is fickle), is so lyrical that Verdi didn't let the tenor rehearse it until the day of the premiere. He was afraid it would become popular before the opening night and lessen the impact of the opera. He was right. Immediately after the first performance, the song, "La donna e mobile," was being whistled by nearly everybody.

The other aria, "Caro nome," was composed for a coloratura soprano. The rapid scales and trills in this aria are designed primarily to show off the singer's voice. The Wagnerians used this aria as a model for all that they insisted was wrong in opera; it was beautiful to listen to, but it brought a halt to the drama.

Just two years later, his second masterpiece, *Il Trovatore,* was presented to the public. The story of *The Troubadour* is so complex and confusing that it almost defies a brief synopsis. It is about two brothers, separated when young by a revengeful gypsy woman. Without realizing they are brothers, they compete for the hand of the beautiful Leonora. They come close to killing each other on more than one occasion, in their fights for the girl. In the end, Leonora kills herself with poison, while one brother burns the other at the stake. Obviously, it is the lovely melodies that make this a popular work.

One year after *Il Trovatore, La Traviata* found its way to the stage. *La Traviata* is a very moving opera, a sad story of a young courtesan who, when she finally experiences true love, must give up that love to spare the young man's reputation. It was one of the first operas to use a contemporary plot (the scene is set in Paris in the 1850s). The opera is filled with melodic arias and duets, love songs, drinking songs, and sorrowful songs of parting.

Probably the most popular opera of Verdi's today, *La Traviata* was not liked when it was first performed, mainly because it was performed badly. The soprano playing Violetta was a huge, buxom woman. The part called for a young woman dying of consumption, and the audience only laughed when the death scene came on, as they watched the big fat soprano tottering around on the stage singing out her death aria. By this time, audience reactions no longer bothered Verdi. "I know this opera is good," he said. "And someday they will know it."

The Song is Supreme

The greatest influence on Verdi was the Italian version of *bel canto* (beautiful song). Creating beautiful melodies to be sung as arias and duets was of first importance as far as Verdi was concerned, even at the cost of interfering with the story line. Even in his later operas, when he emulated Wagner, his rich orchestral tones were still highly melodic in character, though they follow the drama in a fluid lyrical line.

Verdi knew that beautiful tunes alone could not insure the lasting success of an opera. He worked hard on the drama, getting his librettists to do the best they could with the melodramas that were in such demand. Wherever the drama was weak, he would skillfully use the music to fill in and carry over the emotion.

He was as bad (or should we say as good) as Wagner when it came to directing his own work: everything had to be perfect, and no one, not even the greatest prima donna, was exempt from his wrath when one of the scenes was not done just the way he wanted it. Unlike Wagner, Verdi would not discuss his theories of opera. "I create my work, the public usually likes it. That's theory enough."

Verdi was soon so popular that his operas were not only playing in every major city, but several theaters in each city were producing Verdi works. No matter how much the public liked his compositions, Verdi still had a lot of trouble with music critics, especially the critics outside of Italy. They felt his music was to simple, just one obvious melody after another. "His appeal is only temporary," they insisted. "Such songs seldom have lasting value." Verdi just laughed at them. "The day of justice for them will come," he said, "and nothing gives an artist more pleasure than being able to say: 'Imbeciles, you were wrong!'"

Keeping the Faith

Italy was out of the mainstream of the many changes that were taking place in the art world, yet it remained a center of culture throughout the nineteenth century. Paris was the greatest city of contemporary music and art, but Rome represented all that was traditional and fundamental in the art world. The most treasured prize at the Paris Conservatory was the Prix de Rome, a three-year scholarship to study music in Italy (Berlioz, you will remember, tried five times before he finally won this prize).

Though many European artists traveled to Italy to receive training in their discipline, having Italy as the center of tradition was not good for the Italian artists themselves. They were trapped by their own traditions. They were giving to the rest of Europe, but receiving little in return. While London, Paris, Vienna, and St. Petersburg produced new and progressive artists, Italy kept reproducing artists from the same mold. In the 1860s, when nationalism was sweeping Italy (it was in this decade that the various Italian states would finally be united), a group of painters calling themselves "Machiaioli" (The Rogues) began to emulate the French and English painters who were paving new ways in art with their experiments with color and light. They were especially influenced by the French artist, Jean Baptiste Corot, who visited Italy several times and became good friends with several of the Machiaioli.

The Machiaioli were still cautious in their artistic expressions, and they never broke completely from their more conservative fellow artists. There was nothing in Italy during the nineteenth century comparable to the upheavals in the art world taking place in the rest of Europe: no impressionist movement, no pointillists, no individual like Toulouse-Lautrec, whose work defies categorizing. It wasn't until the end of the century, at the Biennale in Venice in 1895, that the Italian artists were introduced to the French Symbolists.

There were some artists, though, besides the composers, who created in the new manner. The sculptor Medardo Rosso, working mainly with highly malleable materials like plaster and wax, sculpted impressionistic works very much like those by the French sculptor August Rodin. In his plaster bust, "The Portrait of Madame Noblet," Rosso purposely left one side of the subject's face blurred, to give the impression that the face was partly in shadow. Toward the end of his life, Rodin, who was the most original sculptor in Europe, was said to be envious of some of Rosso's impressionistic works.

The nineteenth century was not one of artistic experimentation for Italians in general. There are very few names besides Rosso and Verdi that can be placed among the great names of the other European romantics.

The Politician and the Plow

Verdi lived in an Italy that was subjugated to the Austrians. Along with many other Italian patriots, Verdi resented Austrian rule and longed for Italian independence. Verdi used his operas to make his political opinions known. In doing so, he defied the Austrian censors, who read every play. To Verdi, the constant trouble with them was worth it, for he was able to raise the hope of his audience that one day Italy would again be free.

Verdi's very name symbolized the Italian revolution: *Vittorio Emmanuele, Re d'Italia*. When people shouted "Viva, Verdi" in the theaters, they were shouting "Long Live Vittorio Emmanuele, King of Italy."

Verdi's next opera, *Un Ballo in Maschera* (The Masked Ball), again showed his patriotic concerns. He was forced to change the setting for this opera from Sweden to Boston, because the Austrian authorities were upset by his attacks on royalty. Instead of King Riccardo getting killed, it would be the governor of Boston. It was perfectly all right to murder an American.

Most modern versions of this opera are performed the way Verdi first wrote it, with a European king getting stabbed instead of an American governor.

In 1860, the Kingdom of Italy finally became a reality. Within a few years, Venice was free from Austrian rule too, and by 1870, the Italian hero Garibaldi had secured the freedom of Sicily and Naples.

When the Italian parliament was reestablished in a united Italy, Verdi was overwhelmingly elected to it as a deputy. He served his country well, although he did not like being a politican. "They are worse than the prima donnas in the theater," he complained. In 1874, the King of Italy honored Verdi by appointing him Senator, a position that did not require his constant presence in the parliament.

Verdi preferred a different life. He had remarried, twenty years after Margherita's death, and was once more finding personal happiness. He bought a farm near Busseto and spent as much time there as possible. "I would have been just as happy as a farmer," he said; and it was true. He managed to bring in profitable crops, and helped bring a prosperity to his village that was unique at the time. When a downturn in Italy's economics resulted in a large-scale emigration to America, Verdi was proud to report that all his villagers could be employed by his farm and not be forced to leave their country.

He had many visitors. His friends from the art world and from the Italian senate liked to relax in the country atmosphere. Verdi still managed to keep his worlds separate. "The only piano you'll find here," he warned his visitors, "is one with broken strings. So keep the conversation to the subject of crops."

Grand Opera

Verdi's last opera in the *bel canto* style was commissioned by the Khedive of Egypt to celebrate the opening of the Suez Canal in the 1870s, and it had its premiere in the new Egyptian house. *Aida* is Grand Opera, filled with beautiful and spectacular scenes, such as the Grand March in the second act and the tomb scene at the end. One of the most beautiful arias for tenor opens the first act. Radames, an Egyptian soldier, is in love with the slave girl, Aida. In "Celeste (heavenly) Aida," he sings of his love and vows to someday make her a queen. In a war against the invading Ethiopians, Radames captures Aida's father and finds himself in an impossible situation. Aida wants him to release her father, but to do so would mean another war. At her father's prompting, Aida gets Radames to tell her of the Egyptian army's military plans. He is caught, and for his treason, he is sentenced to death. He is to be buried alive in a tomb beneath the earth. Aida, unknown to anyone, hides in the tomb and shares Radames's fate when it is sealed. The opera ends as the two lovers sing a stirring duet, "O terra, addio," Oh world, farewell.

Aida was a resounding success in Egypt, to the extent that the audience kept interrupting the opera with cheers and applause. The newspapers and the people wondered what Verdi would create next.

After finishing *Aida,* however, fifteen years would go by before Verdi would write another opera. He felt that the new style of opera writing, Wagnerian music dramas, required a way of thought and expression that were foreign to him. Thus, instead of writing more operas in the "old" style, which he himself believed was outdated, he would not compose any operas at all.

Verdi and Wagner were wrong: they both believed that Verdi's style was outdated. The public has never agreed with that observation, and apparently never will. Verdi's operas are performed more than anyone else's. *La Traviata* alone has been performed more than all of Wagner's operas put together; and the same is possibly true of *Il Trovatore* and *Rigoletto*.

Verdi was almost sixty years old at the time of *Aida* and he was tired. His place in Italian musical history was without precedent. For more than thirty years he had reigned supreme. There was no one, absolutely no one, who could challenge him. That was the best time to retire, he thought, when he was on top.

Boito and the New Beginning

For ten years, Verdi refrained from composing any more operas. Then in 1879, he met a young poet and librettist named Arriog Boito. Boito was born when Verdi was already thirty years old; he was of a different generation, and his ideas about music and art reflect this difference. A devoted fan of Wagner's music dramas, Boito wrote many articles attacking the present state of Italian opera and suggested that the composers in his country pay more attention to the Wagnerian "Music of the Future."

This did not endear him to Verdi. "Italian art is not German art," he insisted. "We cannot and we should not compose like the Germans, nor they like us."

But Boito persisted. He himself could only complete one opera. He was so caught up between his own Italian heritage and the desire to be one with the German spirit, that it kept him from doing the many things he dreamed of and insisted that other composers do. Also, the failure of his one opera, *Mefistofele* (which was popular only in Italy), had a bad effect on his creative nature. He was able only to write poetry and opera librettos. One day he offered a libretto on Shakespeare's *Othello* to Verdi.

Verdi was reluctant to read it, he didn't like Boito, and he had no intention of composing the music for the libretto. He had not counted on Boito's persistence and his poetry. He finally read *Othello*, and it inspired the older man to return to composing.

Verdi was very fussy though, and Boito's patience was tested time and again. The idea for the opera first came up in 1879, but it was 1887, a matter of eight long years of optimistic work, before the first performance took place.

With *Othello*, in both script and music, Verdi moved from melodrama to drama. The music was made to flow as melodically as his previous works, but there were only a few songs that broke away from the action and could be considered true arias. The drama was kept foremost in mind, and the music was composed to underscore and add brilliant tone color to Shakespeare's play. The coming together in this opera of Verdi's great lyrical talent with the Wagnerian style, caused a sensation in both Europe and America, where these two giants of opera had long been considered irreconcilable. *Othello* was a great success, and the public was again wondering what Verdi would do next.

The Second Time Around

Despite the success of *Othello*, Verdi again resolved to write no more operas. He had shown that he could compose in the new style, creating music dramas in the Wagnerian fashion. Now he just wanted to rest.

Then Boito paid him another visit, this time with the story of Falstaff, another libretto based on Shakespeare. Verdi was again so enchanted by Boito's poetry and drama that he could not keep himself from composing the music for it.

Verdi could only work for two or three hours a day on his last opera, *Falstaff*. He kept at it from 1889 until he was finished in 1893, when he was eighty years old. There are arias and ensembles in *Falstaff*, but, as in *Othello*, they are kept wedded to the main score. There are certainly few long arias which call attention to themselves. Falstaff's "Quand'ero paggio" takes less than half a minute to sing; Nannetta and Fenton's duet takes less than two minutes. Verdi integrated the vocal music as much as he could into the story line.

In 1893, *Falstaff* was produced at La Scala Opera House, and again, Verdi had scored a great success, his last, though, for sure.

The Golden Light

Though Verdi's operas did move toward the style of Wagner's music dramas, he insisted on a distinct difference between them. "There is a bright golden light in Italian music," he said, that was not to be found in German compositions. "Let us never lose that golden light."

The light in his own private life was dimming, though. He lived alone in his last years, staying in Milan after his second wife died. He used some of his money to establish a Musicians' Rest Home, where aged and infirmed musicians could find some care and comfort in their last days. He endowed the home with enough money to keep it going for thirty years.

One day in his eighty-seventh year, he suffered a paralytic stroke. He fought against death for six days, but finally, on January 27, 1901, he died. Italy so grieved, that the schools were closed for the day, and speeches were given in the Senate praising the works of the great composer. He was buried quietly without the public looking on, and without a single note of music played over him. Those were his wishes. He would go to Margherita in silence.

No Need to Innovate

In comparison with the other romantic composers in Europe, Verdi added very little to the period in the way of changes or developments. He did for the Italian orchestra what Berlioz had done in France, enlarging it and getting greater tone colors; but that was not his own innovation, he was simply following Berlioz' example. Not until late in life, did he experiment with the dramatic aspects of his operas. Even then, he was following in the footsteps of Wagner.

Verdi was not an innovator. Yet he was still a great romantic. No other composer was as close to the land and nature as Verdi; no other romantic suffered the despair that the terrible loss of his wife and children brought (Berlioz' melodramatics over Harriet Smithson seem ludicrous in comparison); and no other composer was as much a patriot and freedom lover as Verdi, Chopin included.

While it is true that Verdi's fight for political freedom was not carried over into his aesthetics, he was content to use the operatic forms of the past, his feelings for nature, his understanding of grief and suffering, his yearnings for a free and united homeland, and his marvelous ear for tonal color combined to give Verdi the power to compose the most beautiful and stirring vocal music ever written. In this lies his greatest contribution to the romantic period.

Study Activities

1. Listen to some arias from Verdi's early operas, *Rigoletto, La Traviata,* etc. Why are the vocal parts for opera so different from popular and folk singing? Does one require more talent, training (or both) than the other? Is it snobbish or truthful (or both) to say that opera is a more developed form of art than rock music? Which do you think you could more easily master?

2. Compare Boito's opera *Mefistofele* with Gounod's opera *Faust.* Both are based on Goethe's play. What are some of the differences between the two versions? What scenes from the play are not in the operas? What scenes and characters in the operas are given more emphasis than they receive in the play? What accounts for these differences?

3. Verdi was a politician as well as an artist. Are there any artists in our time (musicians, actors, painters, etc.) involving themselves in politics? Do you think they should? What expertise do they bring to politics?

4. Match the names with the appropriate tool or object:

Rodin	Easel
Van Gogh	Manuscript
Balzac	Rhymes
Degas	Armature
Arnold	Chisels
Rosso	Oils

X

Peter Tchaikovsky:
The Heart of Russia

Peter Ilich Tchaikovsky was born in Russia in 1840. The parallels between his life and Robert Schumann's are startling. Like Schumann, Tchaikovsky suffered from hypersensitivity. He felt everything too intensely. He was a "porcelain child," his governess said, "easily hurt and quick to collapse in tears." There was a history of hypersensitivity and epilepsy in his family (his father was an epileptic), and Tchaikovsky would go through his whole life worrying that he would go insane and be placed in a horrible institution.

Tchaikovsky came late to music. As a child he loved music and learned how to play the piano, but his studies were directed toward a career in law. Like Schumann's mother, Mrs. Tchaikovsky insisted that Peter become a lawyer. It wasn't entirely selfish; she feared that music added to her son's instability. Whenever he heard an especially beautiful melody he burst into tears, claiming the music made him "overwhelmingly joyous." Sometimes he would stay awake all night because imaginary music kept going through his head.

Tchaikovsky

When Peter was ten years old, his mother took him to St. Petersburg and placed him in a preparatory school for the study of law. It was a traumatic experience for a sensitive boy like Peter to have his mother leave him in a strange institution, and it awakened all his fears. When she left, the young boy was almost killed beneath the wheels of her carriage trying to stop her from going. He adjusted to the school eventually, he had no choice. He was a lonely boy, and his sense of isolation among the other boys only increased his neuroses and anxieties. When his mother died of cholera four years later, Peter almost broke down under the intensity of his unhappiness.

Music seemed to fill a void in his life. In his last years at law school he studied the piano and spent much of his time attending concerts. He even tried his hand at composing. He graduated from the School of Jurisprudence when he was twenty and, as his mother had wished, he worked in the Ministry of Justice. He hated it.

The Freedom of Choice

When Tchaikovsky was twenty-two he decided to give up law. He went to Anton Rubinstein, the director of the conservatory, and asked to be accepted as a student. It was obvious to the director that his new pupil, even without the proper childhood training, was a great talent. He was right. By the time Tchaikovsky graduated in 1865, he had already succeeded in getting a number of his smaller works performed, string quartets, overtures, and some piano pieces that made his name known at least in Russia.

For the next twelve years, Tchaikovsky taught harmony at the Moscow Conservatory, run by Anton Rubinstein's brother, Nicholas. It was a rewarding period as far as compositions were concerned, but quite taxing on his mental health.

He began work on a symphony. His neurotic tendencies took control when he was about halfway through. The tension and anxiety he felt about his own limitations as a composer and completing such a tremendous task as a full length symphony, caused him severe headaches and insomnia. This, unfortunately, brought about hypochondria, and he began to think that he was seriously ill, even dying from some strange, incurable disease. He taxed his strength working on his symphony, trying to complete it before he died, and in fact, almost did kill himself. The result of it all was that he suffered a nervous breakdown and had to take a forced rest in the country, putting the symphony aside for some months.

Tchaikovsky's *Symphony No. 1,* called "Winter Dreams," was a resounding success when it was presented in Moscow. It was based on Russian folk melodies, and everybody seemed to like it, even the "nationalists" who usually disliked the Conservatory composers. The success encouraged Tchaikovsky, but it did not cure him of his unreasonable fears and lack of self-confidence. He had more successes in the next few years (his opera *Voyevode* and orchestral overture *Fatum*), but he also had some disheartening failures. His two most important works of this period, the *Romeo and Juliet Overture* and his *Piano Concerto No. 1,* were not received enthusiastically. It is difficult to understand why they weren't, they are among the most beautiful compositions in music. It took them several performances over a few years before they fully established themselves. Tchaikovsky even revised the *Romeo and Juliet Overture* in 1879 to make it more musically seductive.

The Russian Five

Until the last half of the nineteenth century, Russian culture was dominated by Western Europe. The Russian elite tried to emulate Parisian manners and Italian art. They ignored, for the most part, their own great Russian traditions and folklore and did their best to be European. It was always a victory for the Czar or some other Russian nobleman to entice one of the European masters to make his home in Russia and entertain and teach them. Chopin, if you will recall, turned down such an offer by the Czar. Others, like Liszt and Wagner, were happy to tour Russia, earning money and reputations while doing so.

A small group of Russians living in St. Petersburg, Balakirev, Borodin, Cui, Mussorgsky, and Rimsky-Korsakov, known as "The Russian Five," called out for a nationalist music. They based their own compositions on the melodies and rhythms of Russian folk music and berated anyone who didn't follow their lead. They especially had it in for Tchaikovsky.

Nothing is sadder than to picture poor Tchaikovsky at the beginning of his career scurrying back and forth between Moscow and St. Petersburg, seeking the approval of the autocratic Balakirev and his band of self-styled critics. Tchaikovsky was delighted when they liked his *First Symphony*. In many ways Tchaikovsky was a nationalist, too. His works were filled with Russian songs and dances, both melody and harmony Slavic in tone. Yet he brought to his work a sophistication and elegance similar to Mozart's and Mendelssohn's and a use of form and orchestration derived from the European composers. It was for this that the Russian Five attacked him. "Russia is raw and brutal and full of power and vitality. Put that kind of 'form' in your music," they challenged.

Tchaikovsky's attempts to please them didn't last. They expected him to work exclusively with Russian sounds, pretending that Mozart, Beethoven, Schubert, and Chopin had nothing to offer Russian composers. He eventually saw them for what they were, well-meaning patriots but musical amateurs not in any position to criticize or even understand his works. He turned away from them, his anxiety about their opinions replaced by a feeling of amusement, something new for Tchaikovsky. He actually felt sorry for them. That helped to restore his self-esteem.

A Small Legacy

The Russian Five were never capable, as was Tchaikovsky, of securing their living by music. They had to continue in their other occupations. Alexander Borodin was a chemist; Cesar Cui was a military engineer and professor at the Military Academy; Modest Mussorgsky was a civil service employee; Nikolai Rimsky-Korsakov was a naval officer; and Mily Balakirev was the only trained musician of the group.

The aims of The Five were good, to develop the music and culture of their own land, but their aims were also narrow. To isolate themselves from the rest of the world was not entirely wise or healthy. Eventually, the Russian Five broke up. Instead of influencing Tchaikovsky as they wanted, he was the one to influence them. Rimsky-Korsakov even joined the St. Petersburg Conservatory, an institution once despised by the group because it perpetuated European traditions.

When we consider the music of these five composers that has remained in the repertory, we see just how right Tchaikovsky was in feeling sorry for them. There are perhaps a dozen pieces by the whole group that are consistently offered outside of Russia. Borodin's music was made popular in 1953 by the American musical *Kismet*. His music was adapted for the stage by Robert Wright and George Forrest. The most famous song in *Kismet*, "Stranger in Paradise," was taken from Borodin's Polovtsian Dances, and the beautiful "This is My Beloved" was adapted from his String Quartet. Wright and Forrest also used parts of Borodin's "In the Steppes of Central Asia," an orchestral suite, for the finale of the musical.

Of the others, Mussorgsky's piano work *Pictures at an Exhibition* is often performed, and, on occasion, his opera *Boris Gudonov*; Balakirev is represented today mostly by one work, his piano piece *Islamey*; and Rimsky-Korsakov's *Scheherazade* is his most famous orchestral work; his operas, though, are quite popular in Russia.

Byron in Russia

One of the writers who greatly influenced Tchaikovsky and the other Russian composers was Alexander Pushkin (1799-1837). A poet and dramatist, Pushkin was the first Russian writer to become widely known outside of Russia. He was known as the Byron of Russia, and like Byron, he celebrated freedom in his poems denouncing tyranny, a rather unwise thing to do in Czarist Russia. In fact, Pushkin's liberal views cost him his job with the Russian Foreign Office, and the censor kept a close eye on him; yet he continued undauntingly to publish his radical opinions.

Pushkin wrote long exotic narrative poems in the manner of Byron. His greatest work, a satiric novel in verse called *Eugene Onegin,* was patterned after Byron's *Don Juan.* Tchaikovsky used this poem as the text for his opera, and he used one of Pushkin's short stories for another opera, *Queen of Spades.* Pushkin's works inspired the other Russian composers, too. Mussorgsky's opera *Boris Godunov* is based on Pushkin's poem by that name, and *The Golden Cockerel* by Rimsky-Korsakov is another Pushkin work.

Pushkin was one of the first Russian men of letters to understand the anti-European movement that was taking place within his country. Long under the influence of European culture, many Russians were trying to establish a culture of their own. Pushkin placed this conflict in his poem *Eugene Onegin.* The hero, Onegin, is infected with Western intellectualism and skepticism; the heroine, Tatyana, who rejects Onegin, embodies Russian virtues. The Russian reading public found great satisfaction in Tatyana's rejection of Onegin.

Pushkin's personal life was no less exciting than the lives of his dashing literary heroes. A moody, temperamental person, he spent much of his time going after the pleasures of the flesh. Unfortunately for him, so did his wife. A quarrel with her lover led to a duel, and Pushkin's life was cut short by a pistol ball.

The Melodist

Tchaikovsky had his own ideas about what made music vital. He was a highly emotional person, and he felt that emotion should be the essence of his music. "There are two things music should have," he said, "the ability to charm the ear, and the strength to arouse deep emotion."

While he was concerned with form, he knew he did not have the architectural skill of Beethoven or Mendelssohn, so he considered form secondary to expression. When it came to expressing himself, endowing his music with passion and life, there was no one, not even Beethoven, who could express himself better. It is his consistency of expression that welds Tchaikovsky's large orchestral works together.

The desire to express oneself is one thing; getting that expression across in the most effective way is another matter. What makes Tchaikovsky's musical expression so outstanding is his ability to create breathtaking melodies. Several of his melodies have been turned into popular songs, attesting to their beauty and popularity. The opening theme from his *Piano Concerto No. 1* was extremely popular as the hit song "Tonight We Love." In 1939, the hit "Moon Love" owed its genesis to the second movement of Tchaikovsky's *Fifth Symphony.* The beautiful and perennially popular "None But the Lonely Heart" was written by Tchaikovsky expressly as a vocal song.

Gynephobia

The confidence with which he considered his work in relation to the compositions of the Russian Five was not extended to his private life. Tchaikovsky was still beset by a number of self-doubts. He had turned to drink for relief and was soon addicted to alcohol. Few people knew he was an alcoholic, but in the privacy of his rooms, he would sit for hours, drinking the whiskey and vodka that would quiet the turmoil in his brain.

His greatest problem was his inability to have a normal relationship with women. He was both attracted to and repelled by women. "I am not normal," he wrote fearfully in his diary. He would be plagued throughout his life by these feelings of inadequacy.

In order to solve this dilemma, he decided to get married: that would make him normal, he thought. There was a young music student, Antonina Miliukova, who had said she loved him. He went to her and proposed. Shortly after they were married, unable to accustom himself to living with her, Tchaikovsky tried to take his own life. Within two months of the wedding, he and Antonina were separated; Tchaikovsky would never again marry.

The only other woman who had an affect on his life was Nadezda von Meck. She was a very rich widow of an industrialist who fell in love with Tchaikovsky through his music. That's what happened to Antonina too, but the widow differed from her in one important way: she never wanted to meet Tchaikovsky. She sent him a letter telling him how much she admired his work, advising him that she had arranged for money to be sent to him on a regular basis so that he could go on composing without having to worry about finances. She insisted, however, that the composer never try to meet her. She never stated why.

It was the kind of unsolicited patronage that most artists dreamed about. For Tchaikovsky, who feared the physical and emotional closeness of women, the arrangement could not have been better. Her generous patronage allowed him to work on his compositions full time, and her shyness, or whatever it was that made her not want to meet Tchaikovsky, corresponded perfectly with his own nature. For thirteen years they lived by this arrangement; she sent him money every month, and he did not once try to meet her, although they corresponded frequently.

Thanks to Madame von Meck's generosity, Tchaikovsky was able to resign from his teaching post at the Conservatory in 1878. He purchased a house in the country and devoted himself to fulfilling his talents.

The Escape in Dreams

Madame von Meck wanted Tchaikovsky to take a European trip in order to get over his unhappy marriage. She provided the money, and he traveled through Italy, Switzerland, and France, meeting other composers and renewing his inspiration. He was lonely, though, and still melancholy. He managed to compose several of his masterpieces during this period, including his opera, *Eugene Onegin* (based on Pushkin's poem), and his *Fourth Symphony,* considered by many to be the best of his six symphonies. This is "our symphony" he wrote to his mystery patron.

His *Fourth Symphony* is in the nature of program music. Unlike Franz Liszt, Tchaikovsky usually did not like to talk about the "meaning" of his work. "I admit that my symphonies are program music," he wrote to a friend, "but it is impossible for me to put that program into words; it would only sound ludicrous. Let the music speak for itself." He was like Mendelssohn on that subject. Yet he did, at Madame von Meck's insistence, write a letter telling her what the music represented. "Happiness is not possible in this world," the troubled composer wrote, "at least not complete happiness. There is some force, call it Destiny if you will, that keeps us from enjoying a full and cloudless existence. The symphony represents the search for happiness." If happiness could not be found during man's waking moments, he could find it in dreams. "One can turn to dreams to find happiness. And how sweet it is to escape life's harshness in a dream."

The first movement of the symphony is both harsh (the horns and bassoons) and tender (the clarinets), representing the struggle with life and the eventual escape in dreams.

The second movement is scored mainly for woodwinds and strings playing a beautiful Russian melody. The music builds up slowly in intensity until the full orchestra is speaking, and then the Russian song re-appears in the strings.

The third movement is rather unique in symphonic literature. The strings play alone in pizzicato. The strings are plucked rather than bowed. Then the woodwinds play alone. Finally, the different sections of the orchestra toss short musical phrases back and forth. The sounds and tone colors are both interesting and effective.

In the last movement, the Russian folk song "The Birch Tree" is played by the woodwinds after a fiery opening by the percussion and string section. The full orchestra is brought to bear in a rousing middle section. "There is happiness somewhere," wrote Tchaikovsky about this movement. "Perhaps it is in the people around you. Rejoice in their happiness if you can find none of your own."

Russian Barbarism

When he returned from his trip, Tchaikovsky settled down in his country home. He tried to regiment his life to some degree in order to get as much work accomplished as possible. He rose every morning at eight and had breakfast. Around nine he would settle in a comfortable chair and read the newspaper. Then he would write letters; he had a large correspondence and answered everybody personally. He usually had a book to finish reading; when he finished it he would spend a few hours playing the piano. By then it was time for lunch.

He liked to spend each afternoon walking out in the woods and fields. He carried a notebook with him, jotting down any musical thoughts that came to mind. He returned to the house at 4:30 for tea, then went to his room to compose for three or four hours. After a late supper he liked to play cards with some friends or go to the theater or concert hall. He would have a few drinks during the evening, and then much later, alone in his bedroom, he would drink enough to put him into a deep sleep.

The years of 1878 through 1881 were extremely productive. Among the many works composed in this period were the *Violin Concerto* and the *1812 Overture*.

Tchaikovsky's *Violin Concerto,* the most exciting ever written for the violin, was first performed in 1881 in Vienna. None of his works gave him as much heartache as his concerto. When he first composed it in 1878, he had his friend Joseph Kotek, a virtuoso on the violin, advise him about the solo part. Kotek seemed to like it. But later that year, when the concerto was finished Kotek refused to play it. One violinist after another looked through the score and claimed that it was too difficult, that the solo part was unplayable.

"Will no one play this child of my imagination?" the rejected composer mourned. When it was at last given a performance, the Viennese audience and critics responded strongly against it. "Too savage!" they declared. "Russian barbarism!" They were reacting to the intensity of emotion that the solo violin attempts to portray, and the very hard and concentrated bowing required of the violinist to get at that emotion.

By 1882 the concerto was making its own way. It was cheered first in London and eventually all over the world. Tchaikovsky had the pleasure of proving the music critics wrong.

The 1812 Overture

This exciting composition was planned to celebrate the opening of the Moscow Arts-and-Industry Exhibition in 1881, and to help inaugurate the great Moscow Cathedral which was to be dedicated that year. The Cathedral was built to commemorate the 1812 Russian victory over Napoleon Bonaparte and the French army. Tchaikovsky created appropriately grand martial music for the occasion.

Because the music would be performed outdoors, he decided to give the people an extravaganza, a real Russian spectacular. He scored the overture for a huge orchestra and wrote in extra parts for military brass bands. He then intended to surround the orchestra by dozens of cannon. He had a special wire attached to the cannon which he could operate from the conductor's podium. At the right moment in the overture, when the music was sounding out the battle, he would fire off the blank artillery. He also decided to place an assistant in the Cathedral, and several young boys in the other churches nearby, to start ringing the church bells toward the end of the overture. He would recapture entirely the glorious moments in 1812 when the Russian people celebrated their victory over the French tyrant.

Alas, all that preparation was for nothing. The authorities decided to dedicate the church with a little more religious solemnity than Tchaikovsky offered. He wound up with an unperformed extravaganza on his hands. It would be a year before he could get his overture performed; that was in 1882, during the Second Moscow Exhibit. And then, it was performed without benefit of cannon and bells.

The music is probably the best tonal painting ever composed. This is one piece of program music that is obvious. To represent the battling armies, Tchaikovsky used the Russian National Anthem and the French "Marseillaise." As the French move their armies through Russia toward Moscow, the "Marseillaise" rings out triumphantly. Then the Russian Anthem is heard struggling against the French. Moscow is ablaze with flame as the two armies clash (the cannons are shot off at this point). As the French finally retreat, the music is wild with Russian songs, and the church bells ring out the victory.

The Hiatus

Another of his program works was his *Manfred Symphony*. This was composed as a symphony in four "pictures," based on Byron's story of the Faust-like Manfred. Like the other two troubled geniuses of the romantic period, Schumann and Berlioz, Tchaikovsky felt an affinity with Manfred, with the inner doubts and despair of that heroic figure. He gave his music a distinct program, titling each of the movements. The first is "Manfred in the Alps." This movement is filled with passionate outcries by the woodwinds, depicting Manfred's feelings about death. The second movement describes "The Witch of the Alps" appearing to Manfred beneath the "Cataract Rainbow." This and the "Pastorale" movement which follows, attempts to capture the feeling of nature, a nature which fails to bring peace to Manfred. The last movement is demoniac, describing the "Underground Palace of Arimanes." Only in death does Manfred find peace, and the symphony ends on a quiet resigned note.

For several years Tchaikovsky found himself frustrated as a composer. "I just don't have any new ideas," he wrote. It was a very unhappy time for him. He drank even more heavily and did a great deal of traveling, moving from one European city to another, hoping to get inspired again. Though he was having trouble creating new works, his previous compositions had thoroughly established his reputation as one of the outstanding composers of all time. In appreciation of the honor that he had brought to Russia, the Czar ordered a pension for Tchaikovsky that would be given to him for life.

Finally, when Tchaikovsky did produce another work, his *Fifth Symphony*, presented in St. Petersburg in 1888, it was a failure, convincing him more than ever that he was through as a composer. Despite the delicate scoring in the first movement of his new symphony, the soaring melodies in the second movement, and the rich orchestration and expressionism of the finale, the St. Petersburg audience remained cool in its reception of the work. They preferred the less solemn *Fourth Symphony;* but then, so did Tchaikovsky. In a letter to von Meck he wrote: "I compared this new one to "our" symphony (No. 4). What a difference! How immeasurably inferior it is! It is very, very sad!" Most symphonies pale in comparison to Tchaikovsky's *Fourth,* so it was not a fair comparison.

He was soon to receive one of the greatest disappointments of his life. In 1890, after thirteen years of friendship and support, the mysterious Madame von Meck wrote Tchaikovsky her final letter. She could no longer send him money, she wrote, because she had experienced financial reverses. Tchaikovsky immediately responded. The money he was getting from his compositions and the government pension were more than enough for him. Perhaps he could help her now. At the very least, he pleaded, they should continue to write to each other. There was no reply. He wrote again, and then again, but for reasons unknown to this day, she had chosen to end their association as spontaneously and as mysteriously as it had begun.

For Tchaikovsky, who never heard from Madame von Meck again, the loss of her letters was like the loss of a lifeline. He felt completely adrift without her friendship, and his neuroses increased with each day that passed.

Sin and Salvation

Like Tchaikovsky, the Russian writer Feodor Dostoyevsky (1821-1881) suffered from illnesses, both physical and mental. He was not as fortunate as the composer financially, and had to endure miserable poverty. There was something in the romantic temperament, though, that thrived on adversity. Dostoyevsky did thrive; at least his art did. Along with Pushkin and Tolstoy, he ranks as the finest writer produced by Russia in the nineteenth century. And like these other writers, Dostoyevsky was a confirmed Slavophile, convinced that Russian ideas and culture would eventually lead the way to a better world.

Like many other romantics, Dostoyevsky was also a revolutionary. He was not as lucky as Wagner and Hugo, who escaped capture and were able to lead a normal life in some other country. Dostoyevsky was caught by the Czar's police and was sentenced to be shot by the firing squad. Only moments before the shots were fired did the Czar reprieve the rebels. Dostoyevsky and his friends were sent to a labor camp in Siberia for five long and grueling years.

Dostoyevsky endured enough suffering for any ten romantics. When he was finally pardoned, he turned to writing and created some of the most vital and memorable characters in literature. In *The Brothers Karamazov* and *Crime and Punishment,* he probed into the minds and souls of his heroes, who, like himself, committed crimes against society and found salvation through a sincere penitence for those crimes.

The romantic's interest in sin and salvation was really an interest in psychology, studying the duality of man's nature and how he is torn between physical desires and spiritual longings. Dostoyevsky was especially interested in these questions, and his writings have often been referred to as "psychological novels." The great psychiatrist Sigmund Freud would later give credit to the writers of the nineteenth century for probing the psychological depths of man.

The American Tour

It is hard to understand how Tchaikovsky ever made it through life as a musician. One of his phobias concerned his conducting. He had the weird feeling that his head was going to fall off. Halfway through a performance he would have to place one hand under his chin to keep his head in place. It was a crazy notion, but there was nothing he could do to get it out of his mind. He knew why he had that phobia; he hated being the center of attention. He was painfully shy, no matter how many times he had gone on stage. "Every new acquaintance, every fresh meeting with someone unknown, has always caused me a great deal of suffering. My shyness is a mania." It is understandable that he would feel he was falling to pieces whenever he had to place himself before an entire concert hall of strangers.

Despite what must have been a horrifying experience every time he conducted, Tchaikovsky agreed to undertake a special conducting tour of the United States. He needed to get away from Russia and his unhappiness at not being able to communicate with Madame von Meck. In 1891, he traveled to New York to help inaugurate Carnegie Hall (he received $2,500 to give four concerts). He also visited Niagara Falls, famous even in those days as a lovers' spot; he went on to see Washington, D. C. He also gave concerts in Philadelphia and Baltimore, often presenting his *1812 Overture,* always bringing his audience to its feet in appreciation. Americans loved his music then as much as they do today. He in turn loved America and her people. "I am very drawn to American manners and habits," he wrote in his diary.

He was then suffering from a severe case of depression. He thought he was only homesick, but when he returned to Russia his black mood only deepened.

Sugar Plum Fairies

When he returned to Russia, the St. Petersburg Opera commissioned Tchaikovsky to write a full-length ballet based on a children's story, "The Nutcracker and the Mouse King." The story is about a little girl who receives a nutcracker for Christmas. She falls asleep and dreams that the nutcracker is a handsome prince. When a group of mice try to take over the toy room, the prince leads the toys into battle against them and chases them away. Then he carries the little girl off to Jam Mountain in far away Arabia where the Sugar Plum Fairy entertains them with a series of dances.

It is a charming little story, and Tchaikovsky composed almost magical music for it, music which is often performed in the concert hall, apart from the ballet. You can get an idea from the concert excerpts what the ballet itself is about. After a Miniature Overture, there is a March (the prince leading the toys), and then several dances: the Dance of the Sugar Plum Fairy, the lively Russian, Arab, and Chinese Dances, the Dance of the Flutes, and finally, the Waltz of the Flowers. It is a light and lively work, enchanting either with the ballet or when played alone as an orchestral suite.

Tchaikovsky composed music for three ballets, all of which are still favorites in ballet companies around the world: *Swan Lake* and *Sleeping Beauty* as well as *The Nutcracker.* What makes them so outstanding and in such demand is his concept of the ballet artist. He treated his ballets like operas, giving the dancers beautiful parts to perform. Each of his ballets has the equivalent of arias and duets, special pieces designed to show off the dancer at his or her best.

In keeping with his troubled existence, none of his ballets were immediately accepted. Like his piano concerto, *Romeo and Juliet Overture,* violin concerto, and last two symphonies, his three ballets had to go through a period of nonappreciation and neglect before they were liked. Each time one of his works was rejected, it added to the already anxiety-laden composer's burden.

The Final Song

In his last few years Tchaikovsky feared that he was going mad. His mental problems were compounded by his heavy drinking. It was a vicious cycle: his many fears sent him to the bottle, and the bottle poisoned his system and caused new fears. Alcoholism so aged Tchaikovsky that when he was fifty he looked like an old man of eighty.

Despite all his problems and numerous neuroses (or maybe because of them), Tchaikovsky produced some of the most beautiful music the world has ever known. He wrote his most moving symphony while he was under the greatest mental duress. He was only fifty-two years old, but he felt that his life was over. He would either die soon or go insane, he knew not which. He did know that he had to finish this one last work.

His *Sixth Symphony,* called the "Pathetique," holds some of Tchaikovsky's most melancholy, and yet richly beautiful, melodies. This is true especially of the first movement which has this famous melody, sung by muted violins and cellos:

He conducted the premiere of his *Symphony Pathetique* on October 28, 1893. Though the audience applauded, he knew that their enthusiasm for his music was not what it might be. This composition, too, would have an uphill fight.

Suddenly, Tchaikovsky felt tired. There was no more fight left in him. A cholera epidemic was raging in St. Petersburg, and Tchaikovsky willingly courted death by drinking several glasses of unboiled water, a sure way to get cholera in those days. Within a week after the lukewarm reception of his *Sixth Symphony,* the composer was dying. In his delirium, he kept calling out for Nadezda von Meck, she who had been his "patron angel" for so many years. She wasn't there when he died on November 6, 1893, but within weeks after learning of his death (she was in Wiesbaden, Germany), the mysterious Madame von Meck suddenly died: her heart had simply stopped beating.

The Culmination

In Tchaikovsky, all the different aspects and avenues of romanticism come together. A world traveler, he was influenced by Verdi's operas, Delibes' ballets, and Schumann's symphonies: a blend of Italian, French, and German that he assimilated so perfectly into his own unique Russian style.

He was a great nationalist, a fervent lover of nature, and one of the most intense individuals who ever lived. He had Chopin's ability to compose in miniature, as well as Berlioz' flair for grand spectaculars; he had the light touch and charm of Mendelssohn; the passionate showmanship of Liszt; the poignant melancholy of Schumann; the prolificacy of Wagner; and above all, Verdi's wonderful gift of melody. His symphonies, overtures, ballets, operas, and piano works are filled with beautiful Russian songs, some moody and sorrowful, others quiet and reflective, and many soaring and triumphant. Except for Beethoven, there is hardly any composer whose works are heard more than Tchaikovsky's. No other composer could have closed out the period more brilliantly, or more romantically, than Peter Ilich Tchaikovsky.

Study Activities

1. Match the composer with his composition:

Schumann	Heroic Polonaise
Berlioz	William Tell Overture
Mendelssohn	Lohengrin
Chopin	Caprices
Strauss	Fantastic Symphony
Liszt	Wiegenlied
Rossini	Symphony Pathetique
Paganini	Hebrides Overture
Tchaikovsky	La Traviata
Brahms	Carnival
Wagner	Les Preludes
Verdi	Blue Danube Waltz

2. Some of Tchaikovsky's most beautiful melodies were composed for ballets. A recent television showing of *The Sleeping Beauty* demonstrated how perfectly Tchaikovsky's music fit the exciting and exacting physical motion of the dancers. How physically fit are you? Try to perform the following ballet positions:

    Arabesque —   stand on one leg with the other leg extended behind the body in a straight line.

    Cabriole —   one leg swings out in a high kick and the other leg swings up to beat against it.

    Tour en l'air —   the dancer leaps straight up in the air and executes a complete turn of the body before landing in his initial position (Rudolf Nureyev can turn *three* times before landing!).

    Pointe —   move about for several minutes on the tips of the toes without losing balance.

3. Listen to a Haydn symphony and then one by Tchaikovsky, paying careful attention to both the form and the content. Make a list of the differences between the classical composer and the romantic (tempo, dynamics, mood, development of themes, etc.). Now compare one of Arnold Schoenberg's twentieth century atonal compositions to Tchaikovsky's composition. Which do you prefer listening to? Why? What accounts for the tremendous difference in sound between these two composers?

4. Refer back to the concluding section of Chapter VI, called "The Romantic Matrix." Using that as a model, compare Wagner, Brahms, Verdi, and Tchaikovsky. Which one, on the surface, at least, "out-romantics" the others?

A Comparative Chronology

COMPOSER	HISTORICAL EVENTS	OTHER ARTISTS
Carl Maria von WEBER (1786-1826)	1793—Whitney's cotton gin.	Francisco Goya (1746-1828)
Nicolo PAGANINI (1782-1840)	1807—Fulton's steamboat.	William Wordsworth (1770-1850)
Giacomo MEYERBEER (1791-1864)	1819—First steamship crosses Atlantic.	Sir Walter Scott (1771-1832)
Gioacchino ROSSINI (1792-1868)	1832—Morse invents telegraph tape.	Samuel T. Coleridge (1772-1834)
Felix MENDELSSOHN (1809-1847)	1834—McCormick's mechanical reaper.	J. M. W. Turner (1775-1851)
Frederic CHOPIN (1810-1849)	1839—Daguerreotype invented.	John Constable (1776-1837)
Robert SCHUMANN (1810-1856)	1842—Ether is used as an anaesthetic.	Lord Byron (1788-1824)
Hector BERLIOZ (1803-1869)	1848—European revolutions.	Percy Shelley (1792-1822)
Franz LISZT (1811-1886	1848—Marx's *Communist Manifesto.*	John Keats (1795-1821)
Richard WAGNER (1813-1883)	1853—Commodore Perry visits Japan.	Alexander Pushkin (1799-1837)
Giuseppe VERDI (1813-1901)	1859—Darwin's *Origin of the Species.*	Eugene Delacroix (1799-1863)
Charles GOUNOD (1818-1893)	1861-65—American Civil War.	Ralph Waldo Emerson (1803-1882)
Jacques OFFENBACH (1819-1880)	1866—Transatlantic cable.	George Sand (1804-1876)

COMPOSER	HISTORICAL EVENTS	OTHER ARTISTS
Edouard LALO (1823-1892)	1873—Dynamo invented.	Edgar Allen Poe (1809-1849)
Johann STRAUSS (1825-1899)	1876—Telephone invented.	Alfred Tennyson (1809-1892)
Johannes BRAHMS (1833-1897)	1876—Internal combustion engine invented.	Charles Dickens (1812-1870)
Alexander BORODIN (1834-1887)	1877—Phonograph invented.	Robert Browning (1812-1889)
Charles SAINT-SAËNS (1835-1921)	1881—Czar Alexander shot. President Garfield assassinated.	Henry David Thoreau (1817-1862)
Mily BALAKIREV (1836-1910)	1881—Panama Canal begun	Herman Melville (1819-1891)
Georges BIZET (1838-1875)		Walt Whitman (1819-1892)
Modest MUSSORGSKY (1839-1881)	1884—Pasteur's inoculation against rabies.	Feodor Dostoyevsky (1821-1881)
Peter TCHAIKOVSKY (1840-1893)		Emily Dickinson (1830-1886)
Anton DVORAK (1841-1904)	1886—Statue of Liberty erected in New York	Mark Twain (1835-1910)
Arthur SULLIVAN (1841-1900)		Paul Cezanne (1839-1906)
Jules MASSENET (1842-1908)	1895—Roentgen discovers X-rays.	Auguste Rodin (1840-1917)
Edvard GRIEG (1843-1907)		Pierre Auguste Renoir (1841-1919)
Nikolai RIMSKY-KORSAKOV (1844-1908)	1898—Curies discover radium.	Vincent Van Gogh (1853-1890)

Glossary

Absolute Music — Music free from extra-musical associations.

Accent — The emphasis or stress placed on one tone or chord.

Accompaniment — The musical background provided for a melody or solo player.

Adagio — A slow tempo.

Allegro — A fast tempo.

Andante — A moderate tempo, between Allegro and Adagio.

Appoggiatura — An ornament or grace note that denotes the temporary replacement of a note by its upper or lower neighbor note.

Aria — A composition for solo voice with an instrumental accompaniment.

Arpeggio — An open chord where the notes are played in rapid succession to simulate the sound of a harp.

Art Song — The combination of poetry and music to create serious songs.

Atonality — The avoidance of a definite tonal center or key.

Bel Canto — A technique of singing that emphasizes beauty of voice rather than dramatics.

Broken Chord — The notes of a chord played in succession; arpeggios.

Cadence — Two or more chords used in progression to end a section of music.

Cadenza — A section in a composition allowing for performer improvisation.

Chamber Music — Instrumental music where there is one player for each part, unlike orchestral music where several players may play one part.

Character Piece — Short composition which expresses a definite mood or character.

Chord — Three or more notes sounded simultaneously.

Chromaticism — Using raised or lowered notes instead of the normal degrees of the scale, e.g. in C major: c-d♯-e instead of c-d-e.

Coda — The concluding section of a composition, often very climactic in nature.

Coloratura — The use of rapid scales, trills, etc. in vocal music.

Concerto — A composition for orchestra and solo instrument.

Counterpoint — Two or more melodies played simultaneously; contrapuntal.

Crescendo — Increase in loudness.

Decrescendo — Decrease in loudness.

Development — A section of the sonata form where the themes are elaborated; fragmentation, modification, and combination of themes.

Diminuendo — Diminishing in sound.

Dynamics — Degrees of loudness and softness.

Etude — An exercise to develop technical playing ability.

Exposition — The initial presentation of one or more themes; the first section of the sonata form.

Folk Song — A song of known or unknown authorship, often handed down orally, widely known throughout a nation or community.

Fugue — A polyphonic composition based on a theme which gets repeated throughout the piece; most often associated with baroque music.

Glissando — A rapid scale produced by drawing the fingers quickly over the strings (of a harp) or keys (of a piano).

Grace Note — See Appoggiatura.

Harmony — Any combination of tones or melodies that interact with each other.

Homophonic — Music consisting of a single melodic line supported by chords.

Impromptu — A composition suggesting improvisation.

Improvisation — The spontaneous creation of music.

Incidental Music — Music written to accompany stage plays.

Key — The main note of a composition, and its related notes needed to complete a scale.

Largo — A slow tempo, slower than Adagio.

Leitmotif — A short theme associated with a character, object, idea, or event.

Libretto — The written text of an opera, oratorio, or musical dramatic work.

Major/Minor — The two basic scales of music, melodic and harmonic.

Mazurka — A Polish dance in triple time with the accent most often on the third beat.

Melody — A *succession* of musical notes (compared with Harmony: a *combination* of musical notes).

Modulation — Changing from one key to another, usually employing transitional harmonies.

Motif/Motive — A brief melody or fragment of a theme.

Movement — Each separate section of a musical composition.

Octave — An interval embracing eight diatonic tones: from C to C, etc.

Opera — A musical drama or play where the dialogue is sung instead of spoken.

Opera Buffa — Comic opera: opera comique.

Opera Comique — A light opera with popular music and a happy ending, the plot usually taken from everyday life.

Operetta — The same as opera comique, but with spoken dialogue.

Oratorio — A musical composition for voice and orchestra with a religious or contemplative text.

Orchestration — Writing for the different instruments of the orchestra, combining their sounds to achieve the desired effect.

Overture — The musical introduction to an opera or play.

Pizzicato — The sounds produced by plucking the strings of stringed instruments.

Polonaise — A stately Polish dance in 3/4 time.

Polyphonic — Two or more melodies played together. See Homophonic.

Program Music — Music inspired by an extra-musical idea, such as literature, history, characters, etc.

Quartet — A composition for four instruments (or voices).

Recapitulation — The restatement of the two principal themes of the sonata form.

Recital — A public performance by a soloist.

Recitative — Operatic singing of dialogue.

Rhythm — The flow of music based on accents and time lengths of each note.

Rubato — Freedom of tempo; taking time from one note or phrase to give emphasis to another.

Scale — A succession of notes arranged in ascending or descending order.

112

Scherzo — Faster in tempo than a minuet, used in some symphonies to replace the minuet.

Score — The manuscript or published composition showing in detail the instruments to be used and which parts of the melody or harmony they would play.

Sonata — A composition in four movements; piano sonatas, violin sonatas, symphonies (sonatas for orchestra).

Sonata Form — Three section form, consisting of Exposition, Development and Recapitulation. These sections are listed separately in this Glossary.

Song Cycle — A group of songs based on one story or a unified group of poems.

String Quartet — A chamber group: two violins, viola, and cello.

Symphonic Poem — A one movement work based on an extra-musical idea.

Symphony — A sonata for orchestra.

Tempo — The speed of a musical composition (adagio, allegro, etc.).

Texture — The melodic and harmonic relationship of a composition.

Theme — The main subject or melody of a composition.

Tonality — Synonymous with key; a change in tonality is a change in key.

Tone Poem — See Symphonic Poem.

Transformation of Themes — Modification of a theme to change its personality.

Transition — A musical passage used to bridge two separate movements or themes.

Triad — A three-note chord in the basic pattern 1-3-5 (C-E-G, etc.).

Trill — Musical ornamentation, the rapid alternation of a tone with its upper neighbor.

Tutti — The part of a symphony where the entire orchestra plays at once.

Variations — Producing a theme with a number of modifications of it.

Virtuoso — A performer who has attained excellent technical mastery of his instrument.

Waltz — A dance in triple time, developed from the Austrian Ländler.